Mary Ellen's

Best of
Helpful
Hints
Book II

Note

To obtain the best results and to avoid damage, the author and the publisher recommend care and common sense in the use of the hints in this book.

Mary Ellen's Best of Helpful Hints Book II

by

MARY ELLEN PINKHAM

Illustrations by
LYNN JOHNSTON

WARNER BOOKS

A Warner Communications Company

This book is dedicated to my hinterrific staff:

Stan Ginsburg, editor-in-chief
Ruta Bruvelis
Steve Chain
George Cleveland
John Jacobson
Dick Madden
June Mattson
Sandy Mattson
Tom Morgan
Cindy Owen
Dana Pinkham
Sherman Pinkham, Sr.
Kathy Rice
Linda Riedl
David Smith, associate editor

and Lynn Johnston,
the creator of the syndicated cartoon
"For Better or for Worse."

Contents

Introduction

We've been at it again to bring you the "best" all-around hints to help you manage that busy life and household of yours. We've had a busy time of it ourselves, testing and reading more than 100,000 hints that came our way last year from all over the world.

We've selected the "best" 1,000 to bring you what we feel is our most "helpful" collection ever—*Mary Ellen's Best of Helpful Hints Book II*.

Happy Hinting.

Part I

Home Stuff

Cleaning the Miscellaneous

A Potpourri of Cleaning Hints

Ashtrays
- Ashtrays (not glass) will be easier to clean if polished with furniture polish.

Ballpoint-pen marks
- Clean ballpoint-pen marks off woodwork and painted walls with distilled white vinegar. First dab it on with a clean rag, then blot. Repeat as many times as necessary.
- For wallpaper, dampen the spot with water, then apply a very light coat of hair spray. Let it set a minute, then blot with a dry rag.

Barbecue grills
- When the grill is cool, place it inside a plastic garbage bag and add enough powdered dishwasher detergent and hot water to cover the grill. Tie the bag shut and let it sit outside for a few hours. Rinse it completely before using it again.

Bathroom bonuses
- Eliminate overcrowded drawers and messy medicine chests by hanging a large shoe bag on a wall or behind the bathroom door to hold toiletries and cosmetics. Childproof it if necessary.
- Or use a spice rack placed at adult eye level.
- Hang a roll of paper towels in the bathroom. You'll quickly find many uses for it.

Ceiling
- Wrap a cloth around your broom head and secure it with a rubber band. Just sweep away dust and cobwebs.

Cutting board
- Scrub it with a solution of two tablespoons of bleach per quart of warm water. Rinse under hot running water. Wipe immediately with paper towels.

Dacron curtains
- You can eliminate most of the ironing after washing Dacron curtains. Add one packet of unsugared gelatin dissolved in plain hot water to the final rinse water.

Doors
- To get at dust on louvered doors, wrap a cloth around a ruler, spray with your favorite dusting spray, and run the flat end across each louver.

Draperies
- Remove wrinkles from draperies: Spray them with a fine-mist plant sprayer as they hang.

Fiberglass tubs and shower walls
- Use the cleaner especially made for cleaning fiberglass boats.

Fireplace
- Clean the smoke film from glass fireplace doors by rubbing on fireplace ashes with a damp cloth. Buff with another damp cloth and the glass will come clean.
- To prevent soot from settling all over the house, dampen fireplace ashes with a plant mister before cleaning them out. Then shovel ashes into a box and cover it with wet newspapers.
- Rub a candle stub along the track of your fireplace screen to keep it sliding easily.

Golf balls
- Soak them in one cup of water and one-quarter cup of ammonia.

Golf clubs
- Rub the shaft and club heads lightly with a dry steel wool sponge.

Humidifiers
- A copper scouring pad in your humidifier will prevent lime buildup.

Kitchen exhaust-fan grill
- Wash it in the dishwasher.

Knickknacks

- Don't dust each knickknack individually. Collect them in a dishpan and bathe them in a little detergent and water. Rinse and dry them with a hair dryer.
- For delicate figurines that can't be washed, use artist's red-sable paintbrush #2 or #4. The long handle lets you get to hard-to-reach places and the little brush allows you to dust without breaking the object.

Light bulbs

- Get more light from light bulbs by keeping them dust-free.

Linens: a new wrinkle

- Store seldom-used linens by folding them wrong side out. Dust won't show on the crease lines.

Marble

- Try covering the stained area with 3 percent hydrogen peroxide. Let it set for several hours and wipe up with a dampened cloth. Marble stains are difficult to remove but this hint is worth a try.

Mattresses

- Use an upholstery shampoo to remove mattress stains. Spray the area with disinfectant air freshener to prevent mustiness.

Microwave oven

- To clean spills in a microwave oven, cover the spill with a damp paper towel and turn the oven on high for ten seconds. The mess will wipe up easily when the oven cools.

Odors: nothing to sniff about

- Make the whole house fresher: Put a solid room deodorizer next to the return vent of your forced-air heating system.
- To eliminate odors in home humidifiers, pour three or four capfuls of bottled lemon juice in the water.
- Get rid of sink odors by pouring a strong saltwater solution or a cup of bleach down the drain. Then let the water run to be sure no bleach remains to erode the pipes.

Pictures

- By using eyeglass-cleaning tissues (instead of a wet cloth) to clean the glass on a small picture, no water can seep under the glass or damage the frame.
- Dust oil paintings every few months with a soft brush. Never rub the painting with a cloth.

Plastic

- When cleaning plastic, try using a rag dampened with lemon oil to prevent smears.

Plastic hanging beads

- Put them in a pillowcase and run them through the washing machine along with a batch of cold-water wash.
- Or rinse them in a solution of warm water and vinegar.

Pleated lampshades

- Blow dust away with a hand-held hair dryer.
- Or use an old shaving brush.
- Or try a paintbrush.

Radiators

- Place a wet towel under the radiator and vacuum excess dust from fins. Blowing down through the fins with the blower end of the vacuum gets rid of even more dust. The wet towel beneath the register collects the excess.

Roller skates

- A good soaking in kerosene will remove dirt and grease from the bearings. Be sure to apply new grease before using them again.

Screens
- Clean screens with the dusting attachment of a vacuum cleaner.
- Or brush with carpet scraps that have been nailed to a wooden block.
- For a thorough job, dust the screens and brush with kerosene on both sides. Remove excess with soap and water.
- Take hopelessly dirty window screens to a do-it-yourself car wash. The high-pressure hoses shoot streams of hot, soapy water to clean off all dirt and grime.

Stainless-steel ware
- You can get rid of brownish stains on stainless steel by rubbing it with a dishcloth dipped in household ammonia.
- Or try oven cleaner. Be sure to rinse well.

Silver
- Use a pipe cleaner dipped in silver polish to remove tarnish from between the tines of silver forks.

Sinks
- Use an old toothbrush for cleaning off mold and dirt around the base of faucets and for cleaning the groove around your vanity basin.

Soap holder
- Use a sponge to hold soap. When you wash, wet and squeeze the sponge for suds—and there's no soap dish to clean.

Teflon
- Remove stains from a nonstick-finish utensil by boiling in it two tablespoons of baking soda and one cup of water for fifteen minutes. After the pan has been rinsed and dried, coat it with vegetable oil.

Venetian blinds
- Use an art-gum eraser (available at stationery stores) to remove smudges from venetian blinds.
- An old sock makes a great dusting glove.
- When blinds are really dirty, hang them on a clothesline and hose them down.
- Or hang them under the shower.

Walls behind stoves
- After you clean the painted wall behind your stove, apply a generous coating of furniture polish. Buff well. The next time you clean, grease spatters can be wiped away with a dry paper towel.

Clothing Care, Accessories, and Laundry

Feet First

The best shoeshine
- Use both liquid and cake-wax polishes. The liquid polish covers up scuff marks; the wax polish adds the shine. Apply the liquid first, let it dry, then apply the cake-wax polish and buff. It really does make a big difference.

More shine hints
- Soften hardened shoe polish by heating the metal container in a pan of hot water.
- A clean powder puff is a terrific shoe-polish applicator.
- And when your shoe brush becomes caked with polish, soak it for one-half hour in a solution of warm, sudsy water and a few teaspoons of turpentine. Rinse and let dry.

Shine in the boss's eyes
- For that quick polish at the office, rub a little dab of hand cream on each shoe and buff thoroughly.

Scuff marks
- Cover scuffs on white shoes with white typewriter correction fluid (available at stationery stores) before polishing.
- Acrylic paint or paint used to touch up car nicks is helpful in restoring badly scuffed shoes.
- Light scuff marks can be removed from most light-colored leather shoes with an art-gum eraser (available at stationery stores).

- Scrub scuff marks on silver and gold shoes with a toothbrush and white toothpaste; the marks will vanish.

Boots
- Make your own boot tree: Tie together two or three empty paper-towel tubes; stand them in the legs of your boots to hold them upright.
- Or use large soda bottles or rolled-up newspapers or magazines.
- Or hang them up with a clamp-type pants hanger.
- Rubber boots will slip on and off easily if you spray the inside with furniture polish and wipe them clean.

Cowboy boots
- Spray the inside of cowboy boots with silicone spray (available at hardware stores) and you'll slip in and out of them without a struggle. (It also holds down foot odor.)
- To prevent cowboy boots from turning up at the toes, clip the sole at the tip of the toe to a clipboard, then weigh the heels down with a few heavy cans inside the boot.

Suede shoes
- Remove scuff marks or rain spots from suede by rubbing with very fine sandpaper.
- Keep those suede shoes looking like new; rub thoroughly with a dry sponge after they've been worn.
- Steam-clean suede the easy way. First remove all dirt with a suede brush or dry sponge, then hold shoes over a pan of boiling water. Once the steam raises the nap, stroke the suede with a soft brush in one direction only. Allow the shoes to dry completely before wearing them.

Tennis shoes
- Clean grimy tennis shoes by rubbing them with a wet, soap-filled scouring pad.
- After they've been washed and dried, stuff the toes with paper toweling. Then dab undiluted liquid starch on the toes and let dry. They'll keep their shape and wear longer.
- When the crepe sole of a washable canvas shoe becomes loose, spread clear silicone glue (available at paint and hardware stores) between the sole and the shoe. Hold them together with rubber bands or tape for twelve to twenty-four hours.

Shoelaces
- Don't come unglued if the plastic tip comes off the end of a shoelace. Dip the frayed end in glue and shape to a point. Let dry before using.
- Leather shoelaces stay tied longer when a few drops of water are sprinkled on the knot.

New shoes
- Sandpaper the soles of new shoes to make them less slippery.
- Or rub the soles across the sidewalk before wearing them.

Wet shoes
- Coat rain-soaked shoes with saddle soap while they are still wet. Stuff the inside with black-and-white newspaper and leave the soap on for at least twenty-four hours. Dry shoes away from direct heat to prevent stiffness.

Tight shoes
- Saturate a cotton ball with rubbing alcohol and rub the tight spot on the inside of the shoe. Put both shoes on immediately and walk around. Repeat until the tight shoe feels comfortable.
- Or purchase a shoe-stretching product from your shoe-repair shop.

Underneath It All

Panty hose
- Have a soft touch: Liquid fabric softener, because it lubricates the fibers, adds life to hosiery. Keep some handy in a leftover dishwashing-detergent squirt bottle and add a dash to the final rinse.

- Panty hose bounce back into shape if you rinse them in a basin of warm water and three tablespoons of vinegar.
- To quick-dry panty hose, hang them on a towel rod and blow-dry them with a hair dryer.
- Instead of storing hose or nylon knee-highs in a dresser drawer, put each pair in a small plastic sandwich bag. It's easy to pick out the right color and the bags are snag-proof.

Got a run?
- Cut the other leg off the panty hose and pair it with another one-legged pair.

Slips and bras
- To rejuvenate dingy white slips and panties, dye them in hot, strong tea until the fabric is a shade darker than desired. Rinse until water runs clear. The color will not wash out.
- How to wash those delicate lace items? Shake them up in a jar filled with warm, mild, soapy water.
- To get the wrinkles out of lace, iron on waxed paper.
- Keep bra straps from falling off your shoulders by sewing light-weight thin elastic from one strap to the other.
- Rub a fresh fabric-softener sheet over slips and hose to prevent dresses from clinging.

Hints for Those Who Wear the Pants

Slacks

- To remove those little fuzzy balls between pant legs, try this: Stretch the area as taut as possible over your knee, then rub fabric with a clean plastic-mesh pot scrubber. Don't be afraid to rub hard.

Jeans

- If you don't want the color to fade from new designer jeans, soak them for an hour in a solution of cold salt water (two tablespoons per gallon of water) before washing them. Use the cold-water setting for both the wash and rinse cycles.
- And before laundering, turn the pant legs inside out to reduce wear from friction.
- Rejuvenate a pair of faded jeans by washing them with a pair of new jeans that have never been laundered. You'll be amazed how the dye and sizing that wash out of the new jeans add color to the old ones.
- To prevent the cuffs from rolling up on blue jeans, fold and crease the bottom of the pant legs and secure each with two paper clips before putting the pants in the dryer. Dry the pants separately to prevent snagging other clothes.
- Or if a denim hem keeps folding up no matter how much you press it, iron on some mending tape just inside the hem edge.
- Rescue jeans with muddy knees and bottoms by rinsing them under the faucet and letting them soak overnight in a plastic tub of water with one-quarter cup of ammonia and one-quarter cup of your favorite detergent. Wash them as usual and ground-in mud should be gone.

Hints to Pull the Wool over Your Eyes

Sweaters
- If shedding angora sweaters are getting your goat, put them in a plastic bag in the freezer for a while before they're worn.
- When the cuffs and waistline of your woolen sweaters are stretched out, dip them in hot water and dry with a hot blow dryer. They should shrink back to normal.
- Hand-wash sweaters in your favorite cold-water wash product. Then fill the washing machine with cool water and add a little fabric softener. Swish the sweaters around by hand until they are thoroughly rinsed. Drain the tub and set it on the final spin cycle. The sweaters can now be spread on towels without leaving puddles.
- After hand-washing woolen sweaters, rinse with one-quarter cup of white vinegar in cool water to remove detergent residue.
- To dry and block sweaters, take a framed window screen and outline the unwashed sweater in chalk on the screen. After washing the sweater, block it to the outline and set the screen on bricks or across the backs of two chairs. Air freely circulates underneath for quick drying.
- Fix a snag by taking a wire needle threader and pushing it through the sweater from the wrong side. Catch the loose thread in the tip of the threader and pull it back through the fabric. If the thread is long enough, knot it to keep it from working loose again.

"Skin" Care Hints

Leather
- Remove ink from leather by rubbing out the stain with baking soda. As the powder absorbs the stain it becomes discolored. Reapply the baking soda until the stain disappears.

- To remove grease stains rub with a thick mixture of Fuller's paste and water. When dry, brush paste off.
- Using cold cream is an inexpensive way to clean and soften leather items. Just rub the cream into the leather with fingertips, then wipe clean with a dry cloth.
- Never put a sticky name tag on suede or leather garments.

Suede
- Clean suede by gently rubbing, in a circular motion, ground oatmeal into the stain with a clean cloth. Brush out all the powder with a wire brush. Repeat if necessary.

Hints to Top It Off

Fur real
- Use a wire brush to fluff up dry, matted trim on fur coats.
- Caught in the rain? Shake your fur coat and hang it in a well-ventilated area away from direct heat.
- Allow furs to breathe. Don't cover them with plastic or smother them between other coats in the closet.
- Put a pest strip in the closet instead of mothballs. Mothball odor clings to fur and is very difficult to eliminate.

Hats
- To reshape an old straw hat, soak it in salt water until it's soft. Then shape it and let dry.
- The limp veil on your hat will perk up after being sprayed lightly with hair spray.
- Or iron it under a sheet of waxed paper.

Gems for Jewels

No more tangles
- Hang long necklaces and chains on a small bulletin board and secure each piece with a push pin.

- Or hang chains on men's tie holders. Fasten the tie holder to the inside of a closet door.
- Or hang them on small cup hooks that can be easily screwed to the inside of your closet door or to a free wall in the closet.
- Or put them in drinking straws, then fold each end.
- Or wrap chains around a hair roller and secure them with bobby pins.

Untangling
- To untangle a thin chain, try rubbing it between your hands for a minute or two.
- Or dust the knot with talcum powder and untangling will be easier.
- Or put a drop or two of salad oil or baby oil on a piece of waxed paper, lay the knot in the oil, and undo it with two straight pins.

Storing
- Egg cartons, plastic silverware trays, and plastic ice-cube trays make excellent storage containers for jewelry.
- Fasten pierced earrings through the holes of a small button so they won't get separated or lost.
- Or line your jewelry box with foam rubber and stick the posts into the foam.

Diamonds
- Here's a formula gemologists use to clean diamonds, rubies, and sapphires: Mix in a bowl one cup of water, one-quarter cup of ammonia, and a tablespoon of dishwashing detergent. Scrub the jewelry lightly with an old toothbrush. Ammonia won't hurt gold or silver settings. *Do not* use this formula for cleaning soft, porous stones, such as opals, pearls, turquoise and coral.
- Or clean gems with a soft toothbrush and Prell shampoo.
- Or soak them in club soda for a while.
- To remove remaining soap film after cleaning a ring, dip it in a small bowl of rubbing alcohol, then let it dry without rinsing.

Gold
- In a bowl combine one-half cup of clear household ammonia and one cup of warm water; let chains or rings sit in the solution for ten to fifteen minutes. Scrub jewelry with a soft brush and rinse under warm water with the sink drain closed.

Pearls

- Soak pearl rings and pins in a bowl of mild soap and water. *Never* use ammonia. Rinse in clear water, with the drain closed, before drying them with a soft flannel cloth.
- *Don't soak* a *string* of pearls in water. Dampen a soft cloth with soapy water and rub pearls gently until clean.
- And to help keep pearls lustrous, gently rub them with a little olive oil and wipe dry with a piece of clean chamois cloth.

Silver

- Soak it in a mild solution of Dip-It coffeepot cleaner and water.
- Or rub silver with dry baking soda and a soft cloth. Rinse it in water and towel-dry.
- Or try rubbing silver with a soft cloth that has been dipped in fireplace or cigarette ashes.

Super-clean jewelry

- After the jewelry has been soaked in the appropriate solution, squirt it with the water jet of your jet oral-hygiene appliance, using clear water. It drives dirt out of the crevices and leaves the jewels sparkling clean. (Make sure the sink drain is closed just in case any gem settings are loose.)

Ring around the finger

- Clear nail polish applied to the inside of an inexpensive ring prevents a green ring from forming around your finger.
- If you have an allergic reaction to a favorite ring or pair of earrings, apply one or two coats of clear nail polish around the inside of the band or to the part of the earring that touches the ear. Before applying nail polish to earrings, clean them with rubbing alcohol.

Ring removal

- Help loosen a ring when your finger is swollen by placing your hand in a bowl of ice-cold soapy water.
- Or rub hand cream around the band of the ring.
- Or rub soap on the ring and finger.
- Or try holding your hand above your head for a few minutes, allowing the blood to drain.

An ounce of prevention

- Don't lose that pin. Cut a wide rubber band to a length of one-half inch. Push the pin through clothing, but before locking it, put the pin through the rubber. If the lock opens, the rubber band will help prevent the pin from falling off.
- Be extra cautious when attaching charms to a charm bracelet. Place a drop of clear glue on the small ring opening to prevent loss.

Washday Wisdom

Lint regulations

- To keep lint from clogging your drain, secure an old nylon stocking over your washing-machine hose with a heavy-duty rubber band.
- Or cut a piece of window screening big enough to cover the bottom of the sink. To remove lint from the screen, simply scrub with a damp brush.

A time-saver

- If your laundry room is in the basement, set your kitchen timer to the length of time it takes each cycle to be completed. Now you can avoid those unnecessary trips up and down the steps to check your wash. This goes especially for apartment dwellers.

Sorting

- Set a small wastebasket in each child's room to use as a mini-hamper for soiled socks.
- Save yourself the trouble of sorting dark socks. Make a small laundry bag for each family member, using dish towels or mesh fabric with a drawstring top. Personalize the bags by making each a different color. Toss the bags into the washer and when they come out of the dryer, the socks are already sorted.
- For faster sorting, mark underwear and T-shirts with a different color indelible ink for each family member.

Prewash treatments

- A bar of Fels naphtha soap wrapped in a nylon onion bag provides the cleaning power as well as the abrasion for pretreating most stubborn laundry spots.

- Remove spots cheaply by applying automatic-dishwasher detergent to wet fabric. Scrub gently with an old toothbrush. Rinse.
- To prevent nylon from turning yellow, presoak it in a tubful of warm water to which you've added one-half cup of baking soda.
- Before washing a garment with a drawstring, safety-pin the string to the clothing. Now you can toss it safely into the washer.

The best way to clean whites
- Pour one gallon of hot water into a plastic container and add one-half cup of automatic-dishwashing soap and one-half cup of bleach. Mix well. Soak clothing overnight, then, in the morning, dump solution and clothes into the washing machine and wash as usual. Add one-half cup of white vinegar to the rinse water. (If you use this formula on nylon or synthetics, allow water to cool a bit, as hot water sets wrinkles.)
- To whiten old or dull white polyester, soak it overnight in a bucket filled with one gallon of water and one cup of automatic-dishwasher detergent. In the morning toss the polyester into the machine and wash as usual. It's a great way to get uniforms sparkling white.

Colorfasting
- When setting the dye in clothing, always do each article separately. Add one-half cup of vinegar and one tablespoon of salt to one-half gallon of water. Soak fabric for one hour. If rinse water still shows some color, repeat.

The best washing compound
- Dissolve one pound of washing soda and one-half pound of borax in two gallons of water. Store mixture in a large plastic jug. Add a cupful for a tub of soiled clothes.

Rinse cycle
- Add a sprinkling of your favorite bath salts to the last rinse water when washing blankets, robes, and spreads. Let fabric soak about ten minutes and it comes out sweet-smelling.
- Keep plastic items such as shower curtains or baby pants soft and pliable. Add a few ounces of glycerin when rinsing them.

Solar power
- An ideal place to dry your laundry in the winter is a screened porch with a southern exposure. Completely cover all screened windows and doors with plastic. When the sun shines through the plastic, the temperature on the porch can reach 75 degrees.

Old softies

● After fabric-softener sheets have been used twice, store them in a jar with some liquid fabric softener. When drying a load of clothes, just squeeze out the excess liquid from one of the sheets and toss it in the dryer.

Drying

● A plastic hanging plant pot makes a great weatherproof clothes-pin holder for the clothesline. When it rains, the water will drain out of the holes in the planter's bottom.

● Does your clothesline sag? Put a link chain at one end, and instead of having to bother with retying, just move the chain up one or two links.

For Pressing Engagements

Wrinkles

● If permanent-press clothes are wrinkled, set the dryer for ten minutes and toss in a wet towel.

Starching

● If you like collars, cuffs, and button bands extra stiff, fill an empty, clean roll-on deodorant bottle with liquid starch and apply the desired amount. (To remove the roll-on ball from the bottle, gently pry the top off with a nail file.)

Dampening clothing
- Don't use cold water to dampen your clothes for ironing. Clothes dampen more evenly and quickly with warm water.

Faster ironing
- For smoother ironing, frequently run your warm iron over waxed paper. Be sure to run the iron over a clean cloth or a paper towel before ironing again.

Lint removers
- Use a pompom made of nylon net to remove lint quickly from clothes while ironing. Brush the net ball over the clothes and the lint will disappear. For handy usage, attach the net to the ironing board with string.
- Or use a large synthetic sponge to take lint off synthetic clothing. This works especially well on polyester doubleknits, which seem to attract lint in the wash.

Sweet smells
- Add a little witch hazel to the water in your steam iron. Your clothes will smell fresh and sweet.
- Or add a few drops of your favorite cologne.

Creaseless sleeves
- To press a jacket or dress sleeve without making a crease, roll up a thick magazine, cover it with a cloth, and insert it in the sleeve. The magazine immediately unrolls enough to make a firm pressing pad.

Pressing pleats
- Hold pleats in place with paper clips while ironing.
- When pleats are pressed, the folds sometimes leave marks on the pleats above. Avoid this by placing long strips of brown paper under each pleat.

Sharp pant creases
- Use a dampened brown grocery bag (with no lettering) for pressing sharp creases. It's especially good for pressing seams on tailored garments.
- For a sharp, permanent crease in slacks, steam-iron them as usual, then turn slacks inside out and run a candle along the crease. Turn pants right side out and steam-iron them again. This method is great for wash-and-wear fabric.

Press on
- When ironing large flat clothing, use the wide end of the board and rest the iron at the tapered end. You'll have more room to iron each section.
- Revive velvet or corduroy by pressing it facedown on a piece of the same fabric.

Stop the presses
- Remove blouses from the dryer while still wet. Hang them on hangers, smooth out at the buttons, and spray with starch. Let dry and pressing is eliminated.

Putting clothes away
- If you could use more help sorting and returning clean clothes to their owners, put up a shelf in the laundry room. Set plastic dishpans on it and label each pan with a family member's name. On washday each person can collect his own clothing.
- Put up a floor-to-ceiling plant pole in your laundry room to hang freshly dried clothes. Let everyone retrieve his own clothing.

Dear dry cleaner
- Before sending a freshly stained garment to the cleaner, attach a note saying what caused the stain.

Storage ideas
- Line dresser drawers with colorful quilted fabric instead of shelving paper. Measure the drawers and hem the fabric to fit the drawer. Apply with double-faced carpet tape.
- Dresses with spaghetti straps will not slip off hangers if you wrap both ends of the hanger with thick rubber bands.
- Used fabric-softener sheets can be reused as sachets in dresser drawers.
- Or put empty perfume bottles in lingerie drawers.
- Did you know that bar soap lasts longer when unwrapped and left to dry before it is used? While drying it out put it in a linen drawer to add a fragrance that will linger.

Going into storage
- Preserve treasured clothing that you plan to hand down by storing in plastic bags that seal. After washing and drying an item, fold it and place in one of the large-size bags, squeezing as much air out as possible. This will keep the bag airtight and bug-proof.

- Worn sheets make excellent garment covers, especially for fur, suede, and leather clothing, which must breathe.
- And don't store leather or suede purses in plastic. Wrap them in old pillowcases.
- Fill those empty clip-on baskets (used in the dishwasher to prevent water spots) with mothballs. Replace the cap and hang the baskets in your garment bags to prevent moth damage.

Coming out of the closet
- To remove mothball odor from clothing, tumble each item separately in the dryer for about ten minutes with air only and no heat.

- Or air clothing outdoors on windy days. To ensure that the clothing stays on the hangers, hang each item on two hangers with the hooks turned in opposite directions. The hangers won't fall off the line. To make clothing doubly secure, clip the garment to the hangers with clothespins.
- After removing your winter or summer clothes from storage, hang the garments on the curtain rod in your bathroom and cover with clear plastic dry-cleaner bags. Run the hottest tap water possible from the shower for a few minutes. The steam will penetrate the clothing and remove most of the wrinkles.

Furniture and Floors

Good-Wood Care

Polishing tools
- A shoe buffer polishes tabletops to a high luster.
- A terry-cloth oven mitt does double duty. One side waxes; the other polishes.
- Chair rungs are easier to clean if you use a discarded cotton sock with spray wax on it.

The best dustcloths
- Add two teaspoons of turpentine to a quart jar of hot, sudsy water. Put clean, lint-free cloths in the jar and let them soak overnight, then wring them out and hang to dry. Your cloths will attract dust as well as if they'd been sprayed with any commercial product.
- Or put a cloth in a solution of one-quarter cup of lemon oil and two cups of hot water. Let the cloth dry, and go to work.
- Capture dust balls from under and behind furniture with a damp mop.

Removing wax buildup on wood
- Wax can be softened by using a few drops of turpentine on a soft cloth. Rub hard, allow turpentine to dry, and buff wood with another cloth.

High-gloss shine
- After polishing, sprinkle on a little cornstarch and rub wood with a soft cloth. The cornstarch absorbs excess polish, eliminates fingerprints, and leaves a glossy surface. Your finger should leave no trace when you run it over the surface.

Out of circulation
- Cut down on the dust circulating through your home by spraying the furnace filter with Endust.
- Or cut used fabric-softener sheets or pieces of nylon to fit your floor registers. Slip them under the vent as air filters.

Turning the tables
- Because exposure to sunlight affects color, the dining-room table should be turned a few times a year to help maintain even color.

- Leaves should be put in the table occasionally. This exposure to light will help them maintain the same color as the table.

Home Furnishings

Wicker furniture
- Wicker will not turn yellow if washed in a solution of mild salt water.
- Tighten a sagging seat by washing it outdoors with hot, sudsy water. Rinse with a hose and let it dry in the sun.
- A paintbrush sprayed with furniture polish is ideal for dusting wicker. The brush reaches into crevices while the polish removes the dust.
- Mildew on wicker? Rub the spots with a cloth dipped in diluted ammonia. The wicker won't become discolored as long as you do not saturate the wood.

Lawn furniture
- Tubular aluminum outdoor furniture won't pit if you apply paste wax. Repeat every year.
- And keep old metal furniture from rusting by drilling a few small holes in the seats. Rainwater will drain out.
- To help prevent moisture damage to cushions, first cover them with plastic, then put the covers on.

Wrought iron
- If rust appears, remove all traces with steel wool or a wire brush.
- Coat with aluminum paint before covering with two coats of outdoor paint.
- A coat of paste wax will give extra protection.

Chrome furniture
- Spiff up chrome table legs by rubbing them with a piece of smooth, damp aluminum foil, shiny side out. The foil will turn black, but the chrome will sparkle.
- Leftover club soda is great for cleaning chrome. Ask your friendly bartender.

Glass-top tables
- A capful of liquid fabric softener in a quart of water makes a great lint-free cleaner for glass and Plexiglas tabletops.

Double-duty sofa
- When it's time to have the sofa upholstered, have one side of each cushion covered with plastic. When company comes, just flip the cushions over.
- Because the seat wears faster than other parts, cover each seat cushion with two sets of covers.

Nonslip arm covers
- Keep all arm covers in place by laying a sheet of art foam (available at art-supplies stores) between the arm covers and the arm rest.

Pianos
- If you are going away for a length of time, crumple some newspaper and place inside the piano to absorb moisture, then cover the top with a blanket.

Sectional furniture: keeping it all together
- To keep sectional furniture pieces from drifting apart, fasten a screen-door hook and eye to the back legs.

Loose caster
- Wrap a rubber band or some string around the caster stem before pushing it back into the leg.

Having a fit?
- Use a rubber spatula to push the material into the corners and sides when fitting slipcovers.

Worn piping
- When the fabric wears off the piping on your sofa or chair, color it with matching indelible ink.

Upholstery tricks
- Space tacks evenly on upholstered furniture by fastening a tape measure along the tack line.
- When hammering a decorative furniture tack, place a wooden thread spool against it to avoid damaging the head.
- Stick a few extra tacks to a hidden spot on the frame so they are available when needed.
- After recovering a piece of furniture, put some of the upholstery scraps in an envelope and staple it to the bottom of the piece. The material is there when a patch-up is needed.

Linoleum

Mop to glow
- Floors will shine between waxings if mopped with a mixture of one-half cup of fabric softener and one-half pail of cold water.
- Or quick-shine floors, after they have been swept clean, with a mop and a piece of waxed paper underneath. The remaining dust will also stick to the waxed paper.

Quick-drying waxed floors
- Dry floors quickly with a portable fan set at one end of the room.

Repairing floor tiles

- A linoleum floor tile may come loose or develop a bulge. Put a piece of aluminum foil over the tile and run a hot iron across the top a few times to soften the glue. Then put a couple of heavy books on the tile to flatten it.
- The same method can be used to remove floor tile.
- To patch a hole or gouge in linoleum, grate a scrap of matching tile in a food grater, then mix the dust with white glue. Fill the hole with the mixture. Let it dry and sandpaper it smooth.
- Or make a paste of finely chopped cork and shellac. Fill the hole, sandpaper it, and touch it up with paint to match the color of the linoleum.

Cleaner mops

- Rinse soiled string or yarn mops in a bucket of sudsy water and a little chlorine bleach as long as the strings aren't coated with cellulose.
- Don't be fazed if you can't shake a dust mop outside. Shake off dirt and dust after placing the mop head inside a large grocery bag.

Clean sweeps
- Dust and dirt collect easier after spraying the bristles of the broom with some furniture polish or water.

Dustpans
- Put a coat of wax on your dustpan; dust and dirt will slide off easily.

Broom care
- Stiffen the bristles of a new broom by soaking them in hot salt water.
- To renew the shape of an old broom, put a large rubber band around the bottom.
- Put a hook in the end of your broomstick and hang it in your cleaning closet. If you stand a broom on end, it might ruin the bristles.
- Cut the finger off an old rubber glove and slide it over the handle. The broom won't fall down if you have to lean it against the wall for a moment.

Carpet

Vacuuming
- A straightened wire coat hanger will unclog your unattached vacuum hose.
- Some vacuum bags can be used many times. When full, just cut off the bottom and empty it. Then fold and staple.
- Save steps when vacuuming. Carry all your attachments in a carpenter's apron.

Vacuuming under dressers
- Take out the bottom drawers from a dresser that is too heavy to move. If the dresser does not have a wooden bottom, the vacuum hose will fit through the opening.

Longer carpet life
- Don't use leftover carpeting as an area rug on your new carpet unless it's backed with rubber. Because the bottom is rough, it acts like sandpaper, wearing down the pile whenever someone walks on it.

Throw-rug care
- Shampoo large area rugs outdoors on the picnic table, then just rinse with a hose. Rugs will dry flat with no clothesline creases.

No slipups
- Throw rugs won't slip out from under you if a few strips of double-faced carpet tape are placed under the corners.

Rugs on the mend
- To repair a rug with frayed edges, snip off the loose threads and dab some transparent glue along the entire edge. When the glue dries, it won't be noticeable.
- Has your braided rug split apart? Sew it back together again with clear plastic fishing line.

The Handyperson

Handy Dandies

Taming of the screw
- If you've already tried loosening a stubborn nut or screw by soaking it in ammonia, penetrating oil, or hydrogen peroxide, try this: Heat the nut or screw with an iron and rap it with a hammer. Use goggles for eye protection.
- Keep a bolt tight simply by putting another nut on the bolt and tightening it against the first one.
- Or put a few drops of clear nail polish on the bolt just before giving it the final turn with a screwdriver.
- A screw will be easier to insert if you push it into a bar of soap first.

No magnetic screwdriver?
- Start a screw in a hard-to-get-at place by pushing the screw through a narrow piece of masking tape, sticky side up. Fold each end of the tape so that it sticks to the side of the screwdriver blade.
- Or glue the screw to the screwdriver with a drop of rubber cement. When the glue has dried enough to hold the screw, put it in place and tighten it. Then just pull on the screwdriver and the blade will easily break loose from the rubber cement.

Avoid smashed fingers
- Use a bobby pin to hold a nail or tack in place as you hammer.

Eliminating hammer and plier marks
- When pulling a nail out of wood with a claw hammer, slip a small piece of wood or a magazine under the hammerhead. This protects the wood surface and gets better leverage.

- Or use a spatula or a bowl scraper.
- To prevent vise jaws from leaving clamp marks, pad them with plastic coffee-can lids.
- Or use a kitchen sponge or carpet scraps.
- For pliers, cut two fingers off an old pair of rubber gloves and slip them over the jaws.

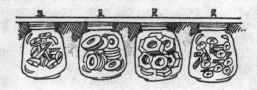

Storing small parts
- Separate nails, screws, bolts, and other small items and put them into baby-food jars with screw-on tops. Then punch a hole in the center of each lid, screw it in place under a work shelf, and screw the jar to the lid.
- Keep nuts and washers together by slipping them over the open end of an extra-large safety pin. Close the pin and hang it on a nail.

Storing larger tools
- Hang a shoe bag with pockets above your workbench.
- Store your circular saw blades in record-album covers and line them up in a record rack. Label the covers clearly and keep rack where children can't get at it.

Storing tools often used
- The tools used most frequently should be stored in an old lunch box. The box is ready at hand in case of an emergency.

Storing tools seldom used
- Before storing seldom-used tools, spray them with silicone lubricant, then wrap each tool tightly in aluminum foil.

A "hefty" apron
- Make a quick apron for those messy jobs by cutting holes for your arms and head in a large garbage bag.

Gluing clamps
- Use a spring-type clothespin to hold a glued object in place as it dries.
- Or use a clamp-type pants hanger.
- And for a very small item, try an old screw-type earring.

Gluing joints
- When gluing a joint, put a strip of tape along the edge. If any of the glue is forced out of the joint, it will stick to the tape. When the job is done, just peel the tape off and any excess glue will come off with it.
- For a stronger bond mix a few steel-wool shavings in the glue before applying.

No tape measure?
- Use string to take measurements in awkward places or around corners. Fasten one end with tape.
- Spread your fingers wide apart and measure the distance between your little finger and your thumb. When you don't have a ruler, this "quick reference" can serve to approximate a measurement.
- If you're alone and have to measure something long with a tape measure, tape one end down with masking tape.

Keep this hint on file
- Clean a file by putting a piece of masking tape over the length of the blade and press down firmly. Pull the tape off and the shavings will come off with it.

Substitute whetstone
- Dampen the bottom of a clay flower pot.

Keeping track of small parts
- Before taking apart an item that has a lot of small pieces, stick a strip of double-edged tape on your worktable. Place the parts on the tape in the order of removal so that everything will be in line for reassembly.

Slick oil tricks
- Put a drinking straw over your oil-can spout when oiling hard-to-get-at places.
- Or after soaking the tip of a pipe cleaner, bend it to fit into any hard-to-reach spot.

Uses for petroleum jelly
- It's a great rust preventive for tools. Spread it heavily on tools that aren't used much.
- Use as a lubricant whenever oil or grease is not handy.
- And apply a glob to the end of a long stick to retrieve a small item from an unreachable place.

Razor blades
- Don't cut yourself when working with a double-edged razor blade. Make a holder by sliding a piece of cork over one edge.
- Or cover one edge with the bottom fold of an empty matchbook. When you're done, close the cover, mark it "razor blade," and store it in a safe place.
- To sharpen blades, use the matchbook striker.

Ladder matters
- Drive spikes through the bottom of tuna-fish cans into the ground and put the feet of the ladder inside the cans.

- And for extra safety, wrap a piece of burlap around the bottom rung. Wipe your shoes on it to remove moisture and mud that might cause you to slip as you climb.
- Tools won't fall off a stepladder platform if molding is attached to the edges of the platform.
- Make a tool holder for use on a straight ladder by wrapping and nailing an old belt to the top ends of the ladder. Then slip your tools beneath the belt before you put the ladder up.
- Or use thick rubber strips from an old inner tube.

Lumber hints
- To prevent moisture damage, stack your shop lumber on top of a couple of old tires.
- Your shop floor becomes a giant ruler for measuring lumber by painting inch and feet intervals on it. Start at a wall so that wall and boards can abut.

Light bulbs
- To remove a broken light bulb, turn off the lamp, then press a thick, dry sponge onto the jagged bulb base and twist gently.

Finding the right switch in a fuse box
- You want to turn off the power to a certain room but you don't know which switch to flip. Try this: Plug in a portable radio in that room, turning it up loud enough to hear at the fuse box. When you flip the right switch, the radio will shut off.

A new way to find a wall stud
- Gently run an electric razor along the wall. When the razor runs across the stud, the tone of the buzzing will change.

Door hinges
- Hanging a door will be a lot easier if you rest it on a small stack of newspapers or magazines while you put the hinges on the frame.
- Remove a door by taking off the bottom hinge first, then wedge a book under the door and remove the top hinge.

Windows
- Stop window rattles! Glue corn pads to the window frames.
- To safely remove a broken windowpane, glue newspaper to both sides of the glass, let it dry, then gently chip away the putty. The pane will come out without scattering glass splinters.

- Repair a small hole in a windowpane by filling it with clear shellac or nail polish. Put a few drops in the hole, let it dry, then put in a few more drops until the hole is filled.

Floorboard squeaks
- Squeeze liquid soap into the cracks.

Squeaky bed springs
- A shot of spray wax will often silence the squeak.
- If springs rubbing against the frame cause the squeak, pad the frame with small pieces of sponge.

Screen test
- How do you fix holes in a screen? For small holes dab them with clear nail polish. Use thin coats to prevent drips.
- Or use a few drops of airplane glue.
- For larger holes cut a patch from a piece of old screen and glue the edges in place with airplane glue.

Frozen padlocks
- Keep an outside padlock from freezing by covering it with a plastic sandwich bag and sealing the top with a rubber band.
- Or cover the keyhole with a piece of masking tape.
- To thaw a frozen lock, cup your hands around it and blow on the keyhole.

Plumbing
- Checking for a silent leak in the toilet-tank valve? Pour some bluing into the tank. Don't flush for an hour or more. Then if blue water appears in the bowl, seepage has occurred and either you or your plumber should replace the valve.
- Put some petroleum jelly around the rim of your plunger to provide a seal for better suction.
- If your toilet is clogged and you don't have a plunger, try pouring six to eight buckets of very hot water into the bowl as fast as they will go down without overflowing. Do not flush between buckets.

Clogged sinks
- Clogged kitchen sinks are usually caused by grease caught in the sink trap. This problem is easily solved if you put a heat lamp or a hair blow dryer (turned to HOT) directly under the sink trap until the grease has melted. Flush the drain by running hot water for a few minutes.

- To unclog a stopped-up sink or drain, run your garden hose into the house and push the nozzle as far into the drain as possible. After wrapping a towel around the hose to fully close the drain opening, hold on tightly while someone else turns on the outdoor faucet. Whatever is clogged should be forced out by the water pressure.

Repairing stereo-speaker rattles
- Take the speaker apart and you'll probably find a crack in the paper cone. A dab of clear nail polish will mend it well.

Repeat performances
- Your appliance or car refuses to make its peculiar noise for the serviceman! Then tape-record one of its better performances and let him listen.

Restoring a picnic table
- Glue leftover pieces of floor tiling to the top. Choose a matching color paint for the legs, and you will have an almost-new table at very little cost.

Get a handle on it
- Make a new pot-lid handle. Paint an old thread spool and secure it on top of the lid with a bolt and nut.

Warped records
- Place the record between two sheets of picture-frame glass and leave it in the sun for a day on a flat surface. When the sun goes down, remove the record. If it wasn't too badly warped, it should be as good as new.

Letter perfect
- Renew the worn dial on a washer or other appliance by rubbing the knob with red or black crayon until indentations (letters and numbers) are level. Wipe off excess crayon and the print will be readable again.

Painting

Hinterrific Paint Jobs

Cover ups
- An old pair of socks slipped over shoes protects them from paint spatters.
- Keep a couple of plastic sandwich bags handy to slip over hands if the doorbell or telephone rings.
- Or wrap a rag around the telephone receiver and fasten it with rubber bands.

A better paint bucket
- A portable lightweight paint bucket can be fashioned from an empty, clean plastic milk or bleach bottle. Opposite the handle cut a hole for the paintbrush to fit through easily.

Eliminating paint-can messes
- Don't use the side of the can to remove excess paint from your brush. Use a straight piece of wire coat hanger fastened across the opening of the can. To hold it in place, bend the wire at right angles, inserting the ends in two nail holes punched at opposite sides of the rim.
- Before pouring paint from a can, cover the rim with masking tape. After pouring, remove the tape: The rim will be clean and the cover will fit tightly.
- Or poke holes around the inside of the rim with a hammer and nail so paint will drip back into the can.

Paint "stores"
- Store leftover latex paint in an empty, clean plastic milk or bleach jug; put the cap on tightly. Shake the jug the next time you use it and the paint will be ready.

- You've got just a little paint left in a large can. Pour it into a small glass jar and seal it tightly. Use for touch-ups and nicks.

Good to the last drop
- A worn-out plastic bowl scraper gets the last bit of paint out of the can.

A stirring idea
- Several holes drilled in the end of your paint paddle makes stirring easier.

Comb and brush
- Run a comb through the brush before painting and those loose bristles won't come off in the paint.

Hands off
- Protect hands from paint solvent by putting the brush and the solvent into a strong plastic bag. Work the solvent into the brush through the plastic.

Right ways to clean brushes
- Never let paintbrushes rest on their bristles in a can of solvent because they will bend and lose their shape. Put solvent in an empty coffee can, cut an X in the plastic lid, and push the brush handle up through the slit. That way you can let the brush hang in the can.
- There's a way to clean several brushes at one time. Suspend them in the solvent from a piece of wire coat hanger slipped through the holes in the brush handles.
- And to clean small brushes, poke the handles through a piece of cardboard, then lay the cardboard over the top of a small can of solvent.
- Give clean brushes a pointed edge by hanging the bristles between clamp-type hangers.

Cleaning paint thinner
- After you have cleaned the brushes, cover the coffee can full of paint thinner and let it stand for a couple of days. The paint will settle to the bottom of the can and the clean thinner can be poured into its original can to be reused.

Shake it off
- The neatest way to shake solvent out of your brush is to squeeze the top of a bag around the handle and shake the solvent into the bag.

Stop-and-start situation
- If you can't finish a latex-paint job, store the paintbrush or roller for several days by slipping it inside a plastic bag, pushing the air out, and tying the end shut. The paint won't dry out.

Ways to clean rollers
- Fill an empty quart milk carton with solvent, put the roller inside, crimp the ends shut. Give the carton a few shakes, then let it sit for a couple of hours.
- Or use a tennis-ball can.

Bugging off
- Have you ever been "bugged" by flies and other insects landing on a freshly painted outdoor surface? Try squirting some bug repellent into the paint before applying.

Painting wrought iron
- Use a smooth piece of sponge. When the piece starts to get tacky, toss it and use a fresh one.

Screens
- Tack a small piece of carpeting to a wood block and dip it in the paint. You'll use less paint, and it will spread quickly and evenly.
- And always dry screens horizontally so the paint won't drip into the mesh.

Stairways
- You can use your stairway while painting it. Paint every other step on one day, and the rest on the next.
- Or paint just half of each step at a time.

Painting the small stuff
- An old lazy Susan makes an ideal rotating work area for repairing or painting small appliances and other items.

Baseboards
- Press down carpeting with a dustpan as you paint along.

Preventing paint peels
- To keep paint from peeling off concrete floors and sheet metal, put a coat of vinegar on it before you paint.

Removing paint spatters
- Very fine dry steel wool will remove spatters from woodwork.
- For spatters on tile and porcelain, use a pumice stick (available at hardware stores).
- To get paint and varnish off chrome hinges and door pulls, simmer them for a few minutes in baking soda and water, then wipe off the solution with a rag.

Keep a color-code record
- On the back of the light-switch plate, write down the color and amount of paint used in each room.

Faster plaster
- Plaster hardens faster if mixed in warm water. Cold water slows down the hardening process.

Homemade patching compounds
- Fill nail holes before painting or wallpapering by mixing equal parts of cornstarch and salt. Add water until it's the consistency of putty.
- An easy way to repair a hole in plaster is to mix paint or food coloring in the plaster to match the color of the walls.

Removing the last bits of wallpaper
- With a piece of sandpaper wrapped around the pad of a wax mop you can scrape off the last bits of wallpaper.

More on wallpaper
- Always apply an oil-based primer before putting up wallpaper. If you don't, the paper will be nearly impossible to remove when it's time to replace it.
- Wallpaper paste will spread quickly and easily if applied with a short-napped paint roller.
- Use the back of a spoon to smooth down a loose seam.
- A squeegee is a handy tool for smoothing the lumps out of vinyl wall coverings.

Marking nail holes
- Put a finishing nail (the kind without a head) into the holes where pictures hang. As you come to these areas push the nail through the paper.

A foolproof idea
- If, like most walls, yours are slightly uneven, dab the corners with a quick coat of paint of the same color as the wallpaper. This will hide any spots where the paper edges don't quite meet.
- Use a plumb line to make sure you're hanging the paper straight.

How to store leftover wallpaper
- Store some leftover scraps of wallpaper by stapling them to an attic wall. When you need to repair a worn spot, your patches will be just as faded as the paper on the wall.

As great as it "seams"
- Before you install paneling, approximate where the seams will join and paint a matching stripe two inches wide. Later, if the seams separate, the old color won't show through.

Lawns, Gardens, Plants, and Flowers

It Pays to
"Mother" Nature

The right way to water
- A little water is worse than no water at all when it comes to watering your lawn. Don't even start the job unless the ground is going to be drenched, and the soil wet at least an inch below the surface. Light watering causes the roots of grass to turn up and become shallow. A thorough watering once a week does a lot of good, whereas light watering every day or every few days does a lot of harm.

Soaking wet
- If soaker hoses will not lie flat on the lawn, tape pieces of a yardstick to the bottom side.
- If the soaker hose is longer than the stretch of lawn that needs watering, shut off the extra portion of hose with a clamp-type pants hanger.
- A coat hanger can be fashioned into a good support for a handheld hose.

Tricks for old hoses
- Punch a few more holes in it and turn it into a lawn soaker.

- Slit sections and, with super-hold glue, attach them to the edges of your youngsters' swing seats. The hose acts as a bumper if the swing accidentally hits one of the kids.
- Cover swing chains with garden hose for a steadier grip.
- Insulate a lug wrench and a jack handle and your hands won't freeze when using these tools during the winter.

Fertile ideas
- Be smart: Buy fertilizer on the basis of nitrogen content rather than price per bag. Inexpensive fertilizer may have a low nitrogen content.
- It's a matter of leverage! Use a broom or snow shovel to move a heavy sack of fertilizer.
- Spread additional fertilizer under trees so the grass can compete with the trees for nutrients.
- Make your own fertilizer spreader from a large coffee can by punching lots of holes in the bottom. Cover with the plastic lid and shake the can.

Hints for mowing with knowing
- A squirt of an octane booster (available in auto-parts stores) will quickly start a stubborn lawn-mower motor.
- To keep screws from vibrating loose on power motors, apply some weather-stripping sealer to the ends of screws. Screws will hold tight but are easily removed when necessary.
- Be sure the blades are sharp. Dull blades will rip rather than clip the grass and cause leaf tips to turn brown.
- Spray mower blades with vegetable oil to keep grass from sticking.
- Unplug the spark-plug wire on the mower so youngsters can't start it when you're away.
- Hang a trash bag from the handle of the mower to fill with debris as you go.
- Wear golf shoes when mowing on a wet or steep hill and aerate the lawn at the same time.

No need to weed
- Why clip the grass that grows along walls by hand? Make a mowing strip around fences and walls to eliminate hand-trimming chores. Strips can be made from stones or bricks placed even with the soil.
- Or dig a shallow trench and fill it with a mixture of sand and used motor oil or strips of plastic covered with dirt.

- If you find that weeds are still growing between your mulch or gravel, try this: Lay plastic over the area and place the mulch on top.

Dandelion exterminator
- Don't let dandelion seeds blow all over your yard: Hook a vacuum cleaner up to a grounded long extension cord and vacuum the seed heads.

Garden tools
- Here's a handy tool carrier! Cut off the top of an old bleach bottle above the handle.
- Or cut it off below the handle—use it as a scoop for pesticides and fertilizer.
- Inches marked off on your garden trowel with red nail polish conveniently show proper depth for planting seeds and bulbs.
- Make a waterproof kneepad for gardening from an old pillow wrapped in plastic.
- Paint the handle of all your garden tools in the same bright color so you can easily see them. If anyone borrows a tool, the color will be a reminder to return it to you.
- Tools won't rust if you store them in a box of sand mixed with old motor oil.
- Use a toy rake to reach those difficult spots underneath bushes and shrubbery.

Tree don'ts
- Don't plant trees too close to the house; they may cause damage to the foundation.
- Don't plant them near a garden where they will block out sunlight and soak up nutrients.
- Don't dig the planting hole without laying a sheet of plastic next to it. When you're ready to fill the hole, just lift the edge of the sheet and the dirt will slide right back in.
- Don't plant a tree in soil that has poor drainage. Check by filling the hole with water. If it hasn't drained in twelve hours, think twice.

Patching bare spots
- Use moss to cover bare spots under trees (such as evergreens). Lay it on bare patches and water it well, and it should take hold.
- If you seed a bare spot on your lawn and don't have a roller, cover the patch with a wide board and walk on it.

Sure shrubbery

- To make sure your hedges are trimmed in a straight line, tie a string to a branch at one end and run it across to the other end. Stand back to make sure the string is straight before you start cutting.
- Keep your pruning shears sharp, as dull blades leave ragged cuts that may not heal.
- Protect your hands while pruning. Use barbecue tongs or pliers to hold thorny branches.
- Put a sheet of plastic beneath the shrubs when clipping. Pick up the plastic for easy disposal of the trimmings.

On the vine

- When putting up a trellis, attach a hinge to the bottom so it can be pulled away from the house when it has to be painted.

An old-seed test

- How do you tell whether old seeds are still good? Count out about fifty seeds, placing them between two layers of wet newspaper covered with a plate. After five days, count the number of seeds that have germinated to determine how thick they will have to be spread. If half are no longer good, use twice as many as you normally would.

Feeding time

- There is nothing better than compost to feed a garden. It can't be bought; it can only be made. Grind leftover vegetables, onion skins, and eggshells in a blender, then sprinkle compost around the garden. Use coffee grounds, too.
- Large plastic ice-cream containers make fine storage bins for collecting compost in the kitchen.
- Pile leaves and grass clippings in a corner and cover them to prevent scattering. As the leaves decompose they create a rich mulch for your garden.

Reflect on this
- If you live in a colder climate give Mother Nature a hand. Walls and fences lined with a reflective surface, such as aluminum foil, will reflect heat and light on the garden plants.

Fast cleanups
- For fast cleanups from your outside faucet, hang a bar of soap in an onion net bag on it. Wash your hands without even taking the soap out of the bag.
- Fasten a broom clip or pound a nail above the outside faucet. Whenever you take the nozzle off the hose, just hang it and it won't get lost.

Chives alive
- The next time you cook with green onions, use only the green tops. Save the bottom three inches (the white bulbs), plant several of the bulbs in a pot and place on the kitchen windowsill. Water daily. As the onions grow, snip off the fresh green tops when needed. They'll always grow back.
- Or use a fresh onion that has begun to sprout and plant it in a small pot to use as you do chives.

Happier ferns
- They don't like to be moved from place to place, so keep them happy and in one spot.

This hint gels
- Dissolve one envelope of unflavored gelatin in hot water and stir. Then slowly add three cups of cold water. Use this mixture instead of water once a month, and you'll see healthier plants. Prepare only as much of the mixture as you plan to use at one time.

Tips for watering
- A newspaper or umbrella held behind the plant protects walls and furniture when spraying it.
- Never put clay pots directly on wooden furniture because water will seep through the porous clay.

Plant sitter
- If you're going away for about a week keep your plants healthy in a homemade miniature "greenhouse." First thoroughly water the plant, then loosely wrap part of a plastic dry-cleaning bag over the plant and around the bottom of the pot.

- If you have many plants, fill the bathtub with about one-quarter inch of water. Set each plant on a saucer so that the pot doesn't touch the water and cover the whole tub with a dry-cleaning bag.

Plants like showers, too
- Plants thrive in the humid atmosphere of a bathroom. The next time you take a hot shower, invite them into the room with you to soak up the steam.

Flower power
- Cut flowers will last longer if you keep them in equal parts of water and 7-Up with one-half teaspoon of chlorine bleach added to each quart of this solution.
- Put a piece of charcoal in the water and cut flowers won't develop a bad odor when the stems begin to rot.
- The plastic baskets that strawberries come in, turned upside down, make great holders for cut flowers in low, round bowls. (Such holders are called frogs.)

To the rescue
- If your local university has an agriculture department, the staff will often provide information and even do tests free of charge. For example, they'll test soil samples or try to solve an insect-control problem.

Part II

You and Yours

The Children

Baby Talk

Special introduction
- Before going to the hospital to have another baby, wrap a gift for your older child. Take it to the hospital and send it home with a snapshot and greeting from the new baby. No one likes to feel left out.

Bedtime
- A standard-sized pillowcase will cover the pad in a bassinet. In case of late-night accidents, turn the pad over to the fresh, clean side.
- Use two or more crib sheets with rubberized flannel pads in between when making up the crib. When baby's bed needs changing, remove the top sheet and pad.
- Hang a picture of a sleeping infant on the nursery door to alert others that baby is napping.
- Pet-proof the nursery by installing a screen door and you'll still be able to hear what's going on.

Temperature control
- To cool a hot baby bottle, store extra formula in a sterilized jar in the refrigerator. Add a small amount to the too-hot bottle.
- Speed up heating water for baby's late-night bottle by filling an airpot or Thermos with boiling water before going to bed.
- Place an uncapped cold baby bottle in the microwave for thirty to sixty seconds for a fast warm-up.
- Add a teaspoon of vinegar to a glass jar filled with water to sterilize nipples in a microwave oven.

Bottle odors
- Rid sour milk smells from plastic bottles by filling the bottle with warm water and adding one teaspoon of baking soda. Shake well and let set overnight.

Bottoms up
- Cornstarch is a good, inexpensive substitute for baby powder.
- Or if you like the smell of baby powder, mix it with an equal amount of cornstarch.
- Use a flour shaker for convenient application but don't shake the powder on lavishly. It can be harmful to the lungs if baby inhales it.
- Or put powder in a clean dusting-powder box and apply with a clean puff.
- Crisco vegetable shortening is as effective as petroleum jelly and does the same job.
- An old card table becomes a changing table if you cover the top with a plastic foam pad. Attach a patterned skirt around it so that the area under the table can be used for storage.

Cleaner and softer diapers
- Soak rinsed diapers overnight in the washing machine in warm water, with one cup of Ivory Snow or Dreft and a commercial soaking preparation (such as Diaperene). In the morning run the diapers through the entire cycle, then once more without soap for a final rinse.
- Fabric softener can irritate baby's bottom, but adding one-half cup of baking soda to the second washing cycle keeps diapers soft and smelling fresh.

Rash moves
- To treat diaper rash remove wet diapers as soon as possible.
- The best place to change the diaper is on the bathroom vanity. Lay baby on a towel with his bottom near the edge of the sink. Hold his legs up and splash with warm water from the basin.
- Because drying with a cloth can cause further irritation, blow warm (not hot) air on baby's bottom with a non-asbestos hair dryer after each change. Be careful to hold it at least six inches from the skin.
- Exposure to air is the best possible treatment. Try to keep diapers off as much as possible.
- Zinc oxide and cornstarch should not be applied while the skin is inflamed. Use petroleum jelly or a prescribed ointment.

- It's a good idea to acidify washed and rinsed diapers with one cup of vinegar and a washtub of water. Soak for thirty minutes, then spin dry without rinsing the vinegar out.

The baby and the bath water
- With a bath towel wrapped around your neck and pinned on like a bib, you'll keep dry during the bath. It also makes an instant wrap-up for baby.
- Don't startle an infant with cold baby lotion. Warm it first by setting the lotion bottle in a pan of hot water.

Helping the medicine go down
- Even the worst-tasting medicines go down without fuss when you put the prescribed amount in a nipple, then give it to baby just before feeding time. He'll be so hungry he'll hardly realize he has swallowed it.
- Give liquid vitamins at bath time. No more stained clothing to launder.

Read all about it
- Haven't had the time to read the newspaper because baby is fussy? Read it aloud while rocking her. She will think you are talking to her and enjoy it as much as a lullaby.

Toddling Along

Fun foods
- Fill a flat-bottomed ice-cream cone with egg or tuna salad for fun eating.
- If your child doesn't like chunks of fruit in his gelatin dessert, add pureed fruit. It's also a good way to sneak in some pureed raw vegetables for extra nutrition.

Fast foods
- Use a pizza cutter to cut up food.
- An egg poacher is ideal for warming several foods at once.

High-chair cleanup
- The best place to clean a high chair is outdoors with a garden hose.

- In the winter place it under the shower and let hot water spray over it for several minutes.

Breaking the habit
- Every week snip off a piece of the pacifier until it's all gone. The shrinking pacifier may make the end easier.
- Or tell your toddler that when his last pacifier is lost or worn out, that's it.

Be a good example
- A simple rule that will save a lot of disciplining in the future is: Never do anything with a child that must be corrected later. For example, don't stand a child on a chair or bed while dressing her. Later she must learn not to stand on the furniture.

Charmin' squeeze
- Little children love to watch a new roll of toilet tissue spin off the roll. To prevent roll-offs, before inserting it on the holder, squeeze the roll together so it's no longer round.

Safety measures
- Perhaps your child, when riding his tricycle on your driveway, rides too close to the street for safety. A white line painted across the driveway at a safe distance from the street might help. Tell him it's the finish line and he's not to go any farther.
- Tie two pieces of yarn to each side of your child's car safety seat and to each attach a favorite toy. While you concentrate on driving, your securely strapped-in toddler can retrieve his own toys.
- Hang a towel over the top of the bathroom door to prevent lock-ins.

Comforting suggestions
- Keep a tray of juice-flavored ice cubes on hand when baby is learning to walk. If she falls and bumps her lip, let her suck on the flavored cube to reduce the swelling. It tastes so good she might forget about the fall.
- Clean a cut or scrape with a red washcloth. The blood won't show and the child won't be frightened.
- Don't apply salve or liquid antiseptic directly to a cut. It's less traumatic if it's put on the bandage before applying it to the skin.
- If you can't see the splinter in a finger, touch the spot with iodine. The splinter will darken and be easier to locate.
- Make a table for a child's sickbed with an adjustable ironing board.
- To help eliminate spills, place a damp washcloth under the plate on a tray for serving children in bed.
- When using a cool-mist vaporizer, the stream of cool mist will be directed where you want it if you tape a three-foot (or more) piece of vent pipe to the vaporizer opening.
- When bathing a child, keep a plaster cast dry by covering it with a plastic bag secured with waterproof electrical tape.

Easy eyedrop application
- Have the child lie down and close his eyes, then place the eyedrops in the corner of each eye. As he opens them the drops spread gently throughout.

Growing Up

Show and tell
- For days when you don't have time to read a story, record several on a blank tape. Don't forget to ring a bell so the child will know when to turn the pages of his book. Label each tape with the book title.

Quick learners
- Here's a great way to teach a child the concept of time. If you plan a trip to the zoo in five days, for example, make a chain of five paper links and have him take one off every day.

- Teach a child the difference between right and left by playing this game. Say "right" or "left" whenever possible in a sentence and cheer if he turns the correct way or shows the correct hand.

Instant clubhouses
- Draw doors and windows on an old sheet and lay it over a card table.
- Or cover the top of an old wooden playpen with a well-secured sheet of plywood. Remove four slats from the side to make a door.
- Or hang an old bedspread over the clothesline, securing it with clothespins on top and small stakes on the bottom, another instant hideout.

Watercoloring
- Put a teaspoon of food coloring in a bottle of water and let your kids spray designs on snow and snow-covered shrubbery.
- Add a few drops of food coloring to your child's bubble bath for a nice surprise.

Finger-paint protection
- Always add about one-quarter teaspoon of liquid dishwashing detergent to finger paints. It won't stop spills, but they'll be easier to clean.
- The key to cleaning these paints off washable fabric is to let them dry. Once dry, most of the paint can be brushed off and the material washed as usual. But remember not to machine-dry because this will set any remaining stain.
- For paint on walls and woodwork, blot up as much as possible with a damp rag. Then gently rub the area with baking soda on a damp cloth.

Fun in the sun
- If your child's slide has lost its "slide," rub a sheet of waxed paper on it and watch him scoot.
- On hot days let the kids cool off in a plastic swimming pool placed at the bottom of the slide.
- Fill an empty, well-rinsed plastic detergent bottle with water for a great squirt gun.
- Carry beach toys in a plastic laundry basket so you can easily rinse off all the sand from them when it's time to leave the beach. Just dunk the filled basket in the water.

Red alert
- For a day at the fair or zoo, dress each child in brightly colored clothing (red is great) to help keep track of them.

Clock watchers
- Kids won't keep popping in and out of the house to find out the time if you put a clock in the window.

Look what's under the bed
- An old twin-bed mattress makes an extra bed for sleep-over friends. Slide it under a bed for easy storage.

Picture this
- Be sure to wash the bottoms of small children's shoes before professional photos are taken. Kids are almost always posed sitting with their legs folded, and the bottoms of the shoes show.
- As the children bring their school pictures home each year, put each one in a frame right in front of last year's picture. It's a safe place to store them and it's fun to look at the whole series every year.

The guest of honor
- The reward for a good report card doesn't always have to be money. Bring out the good china and silverware, set his place at the head of the table, make a cake decorated with a candle for each A or B. He'll feel like a king.

Grow-along clothes
- To get more use from outgrown sleepers with feet, cut off the feet.
- Cut off worn or too-short sleeves from padded jackets to make a fast vest.
- Buttoning clothes will be easier if all the buttons are sewn on with elastic thread.

Winterwear
- To store mittens and stocking hats in one place, hang a shoe bag on the inside of the closet door nearest the entrance.
- Sew a loop of elastic into the cuffs of sweaters to keep the sleeves from pushing up when kids put on their coats. Be sure it isn't too tight.
- Attach some sort of trinket to a snowsuit zipper. It will be easier to identify and the snowsuit will zip up without a struggle.

- Recycle an old heavy sweater by turning it into mittens. Place your child's wrist on the waist ribbing and trace his hand. Cut around the thumb and hand outline, using double thickness. Stitch together, press, and you've got new mittens for nothing.

Happy Birthday

A golden rule
- To limit party invitations let the child invite six friends if he is going to be six years old, seven guests if he is going to be seven, and so on.

Place cards
- Make your own. Write each guest's name in chocolate on a cookie iced in white.
- Or print the name of each child on a paper cup to eliminate mix-ups.
- Or stick a balloon with a child's name on it to the back of each chair.

Free flicks
- Give your child a special birthday treat. Your local library has a fine selection of free children's films. Sound projectors can also be rented for a small fee. Make lots of popcorn and invite the kids in for an afternoon.

Remember this
- Save the front page of the newspaper on your child's birthday and glue it in a scrapbook. It's fascinating to look back at yesterday's headlines.

Family
Business

It's Your Move

A picture is worth a thousand words
- Planning to sell your home in the winter? Make sure you have pictures of its special summer features to show buyers. Take a picture of the apple tree and roses in full bloom or of a family picnic under the shade tree.
- Before moving to a new house, take photos of your old house, your children's friends, the old school, and of anything else the family will have fun looking at later.

Read all about it
- Supply friends with self-addressed, stamped postcards. It's a nice way to hint that you'd love to hear from them.
- While you're still in your present home take a one-month subscription to the newspaper of the community where your new home is located. You'll get a feel for your new community before you move in.

First things first

- Set off a bug bomb in the new house a day or two before moving in. Even the cleanest house sometimes has unseen bugs and this will be your last chance before moving in the food, dishes, kids, and pets.
- Have area rugs and slipcovers cleaned before you move. They'll come back neatly rolled in paper, ready for moving. If you're moving locally, the cleaner will deliver them to your new address.

Start packing

- Label all boxes so they can be taken directly into the proper room.
- Make sure the items you'll want first, such as beds, get packed in the moving van last.
- Cover each mattress with a fitted sheet to prevent damage if it's dragged or dropped.
- Stuff plastic bags with crumpled newspaper and use them as buffers in packing cartons.
- Sectioned cardboard boxes from liquor stores are great for packing glasses and other fragile items.

All the essentials

- Mark one packing box SPECIAL. Fill with things you'll need immediately, such as bedding, light bulbs, a change of clothing, and other indispensables. Move it yourself so it doesn't get misplaced.

Bits and pieces

- Collect all casters, screws, and brackets in a plastic bag and tape them to the piece of furniture they came from.
- When removing pictures, attach the hooks to the back of the frame with masking tape.

Moving the heavyweights
- Put four carpet tiles under the legs of heavy appliances when moving them. Turning the carpeting foam side up keeps the appliance from slipping off, and the carpet side slides easily over vinyl floors.
- When there just doesn't seem to be any place to grip a heavy piece of furniture, buckle several heavy leather belts together and slip them over an end or corner.

Tax deduction for moving
- Remember that moving expenses may be tax-deductible. Keep a file of bills of lading, packing certificates, travel expenses, and so forth.

Maximum Security

Open and shut cases
- For extra window security, drill holes through the frames where the upper and lower halves of windows come together. Put nails in the holes so they slip in and out easily. Insert them when you don't want windows to open, and remove them when you do.
- To prevent a burglar from lifting a sliding door out of its track, put a two-inch corner brace on the inside top of the door.
- Or put a length of wooden dowel or a broom handle on the track and the door can't slide open.
- If you have an attached garage, install a peephole viewer in the door connecting the house to the garage. That way you can investigate a noise without opening the door.
- Another way to keep a prowler out of your garage is to put a C-clamp (ask for it at a hardware store) on the track in front of the roller. The garage door won't budge with the clamp in place.

Cover your tracks
- Make your home a little safer after a light snowfall by taking the time to walk back to your doorstep before leaving. One set of footprints leaving your home could be an invitation for an unwanted guest.

House keys
- The best place to keep a spare set of house keys is with a trusted neighbor.
- Or bury a set of keys nearby in a film canister.
- To avoid fumbling around for your house key, drill a second hole near the edge of the key so it will hang slightly off center on your ring.

Smoke detectors
- When installing smoke detectors, be sure to put one in the basement, too. A fire that starts here may not trigger the other alarms in your home until it's too late.

Under lock and key
- Take photographs of household valuables, furniture, and other items and keep them in your safe-deposit box. In case of fire or theft, you'll have evidence for your insurance claims.
- And make photocopies of your credit cards in case they are misplaced or stolen.

The Family Secretary

Pens and pencils
- When ink erasers become smudged, use fine sandpaper or an emery board to clean them.
- Your ballpoint pen won't write and it's not out of ink? Lightly rub a pencil eraser across the paper and the pen will write more easily.
- When a marking pen seems to be dried out, remove the cap from the bottom and add a few drops of water, then shake it as you would a thermometer.
- And always store felt-tipped pens with the point down to keep them from drying out.

Typewriters
- To cut down on typewriter noise, put a rubber mat under the machine.
- Clean typewriter keys with cotton dipped in rubbing alcohol.

- Vinegar will remove typewriter correction fluid from most surfaces.

At the touch of a finger
- You don't need rubber fingers to thumb through stacks of paperwork. Rub a little toothpaste into your fingertips and let dry.

Drying wet books
- Dry the pages and keep them from wrinkling by placing paper towels on both sides of every wet page. Close the book and let it sit overnight with a heavy book on top.

Underline this hint
- When writing on unlined stationery, put your unlined paper over a piece of lined paper and use it as a guide. If the lines don't show through, darken them with a pen.

Stormy weather
- In rainy weather you can leave mail sticking out from a mail chute for the postman if you put the letters in a plastic bag.

Phone numbers
- Write emergency phone numbers on a small card and tape it to the telephone. Cover the card with clear plastic tape. This can be a lifesaver.
- Make your address book easy to update. Write all addresses and phone numbers in pencil.
- And to change addresses written in ink, use mailing-list labels (available in stationery stores).

Stamp Acts

Getting in your licks
- When a postage stamp won't stick, just rub it across the gummed part of an envelope that's been slightly moistened.
- Fill a used, clean shoe-polish container with water and use the brush applicator to moisten stamp backing.
- Or dampen a kitchen sponge with water.

Ungluing stuck stamps
- Run a warm iron over them, but separate the stamps quickly before the glue sets again.
- Or place in a shallow dish filled with water. Let soak, then pull apart gently under slow running water. Dry them facedown on paper toweling.

Signed, sealed, and delivered
- Cover the address on a parcel with cellophane tape. This prevents the address from smudging.
- To prevent damage to photos, place the pictures between two pieces of corrugated cardboard and slip a hairpin diagonally through the corrugations at each corner. This will add rigidity.

- When sending get-well greetings to a hospitalized friend, write his home address where your return address would normally go. That way, if your card arrives after he's been discharged, it will automatically be sent to his home.

Past History

Kids' stuff
- Store your youngsters' artwork, school papers, and other memorabilia in large boxes in their closets. Once a year, go through the boxes, discard unwanted items, and keep the precious ones. Cover the boxes, label them, and store your memories in a safe place.

Picture perfects
- Store family photos in a file box and use tab dividers to label them by year, event, or subject.
- And put the negatives in envelopes and keep them in the box right behind the prints.
- Make slide shows go smoothly as follows: First ensure that all the slides in the holder are right side up, then run a marking pen across the tops of the slides. Next time you need only look for the mark when putting slides in the holder.

Family lost and found
- A small box in a convenient place may serve as a catch-all for the little things found in odd places around the house.

Lookin' Good

Hand Aids

A treatment for rough, red hands
- Place one-half teaspoon of sugar in the palm of your hand and cover sugar with mineral or baby oil. Massage hands briskly for a few minutes. Wash hands with soapy water and they'll feel like silk.

Overnight sensations
- No hand lotion will ever take the place of pure glycerin (available at drugstores). Apply it every night before retiring and almost overnight your hands will turn beautiful. And to get the most benefit from glycerin or lotion, first soak your hands in warm water before applying it. (Warm water opens the pores and the lotion is absorbed better.)

How to remove super-hold glue from your hands
- Don't try to peel it off. Soak the glue-covered area in nail-polish remover until the glue disappears.

Nail Savers

Repairing a broken nail
- Out of nail-mending paper? Cut a piece of paper from a tea bag to fit the nail. Apply a generous coat of clear polish to the tea-bag paper and press it gently against the break, making sure you also work it under the crack. Then cover with colored nail polish.

For stronger and longer nails
- Apply white iodine (available at drugstores) over the entire nail surface three times a week. If yellowing occurs, don't worry. It isn't harmful and will disappear when the iodine treatment is cut down to only one application a week.

Weak and brittle nails
- Gelatin *does* help strengthen nails! Research has proven that drinking three or four tablespoons of unflavored powdered gelatin mixed into a glass of water each day results in stronger nails within a couple months.

An emergency emery board
- When a nail file isn't available, smooth nail edges with the striking part of a matchbook.
- When the edges of an emery board become worn, trim off about one-eighth inch on both sides and use the inner portion.

Hair "Ways"

Waterless hair wash
- Sprinkle cornstarch or baby powder lightly on oily hair and brush out. To restore the sheen and remove more dirt, put a nylon stocking over the bristles and continue brushing. This hint is very helpful for anyone bed-bound or who doesn't have time for a shampoo.

Formula to control oily hair
- Boil one quart of water with four teaspoons of spearmint leaves. Cool and use as an after-shampoo rinse.

Removing sticky hair-spray buildup
- Wash hair as usual, but work a tablespoon of baking soda into the lathered hair. Hair spray will dissolve.

Out of cream rinse?
- Try a little dab of fabric softener in a glass of warm water. It leaves hair soft and snarl-free.

Final rinse cycle
- Leftover tea makes a great final rinse for brunettes. It will help remove soapy film and leave hair shining.

Dandruff exterminator
- Try shaking table salt into dry hair. Massage salt into the scalp before shampooing. Dandruff should disappear.

Some blues you can use
- Add a bit of bluing (the kind used in the laundry) to the final rinse water to prevent gray hair from yellowing.

Down with frizzies
- When fly-away hair is a problem, rub a fabric-softener sheet over your hair and it will stay in place.

A microwave hot-oil treatment
- For a professional hot-oil treatment, saturate hair with olive oil. Place in a microwave oven, for two minutes, two wet towels that have been thoroughly wrung out. Wrap hair in plastic or aluminum foil and apply hot towels. Let sit for twenty minutes and then remove oil with two good washings.

Believe it or not
- If you lighten your hair, it could turn green when you swim in a chlorinated pool. Prevent this by dissolving six aspirin tablets in a large glass of warm water and rubbing the solution into wet hair. The green will disappear.
- Or rub in tomato juice.

Let's Make Up

Get the most out of your makeup

- Revive dried-up mascara by holding the closed tube under hot, running water for a few minutes. The mascara inside will soften and you'll have more to use.
- Your foundation will last longer if you mix it with moisturizer in the palm of your hand before applying.
- For a sharp point on lipstick and eyeliner pencils, without as much waste, put them in the freezer for a few minutes before sharpening.
- To thin nail polish that has become thick and gooey, add a few drops of polish remover.
- If your blushing powder has broken, crumble and smash it thoroughly. Then keep it in a small, wide-mouthed jar for future use.
- Stretch your dusting or face powder by mixing it with an equal amount of cornstarch.
- Instead of costly makeup brushes use high-quality artist's brushes.

The best makeup remover

- Vegetable shortening (such as Crisco) is an economical and very effective makeup remover. Massage it into skin and wipe off with tissue.

Makeup organizers

- Unclutter your dressing table by putting the cosmetics on a lazy Susan or purchase a two-tiered turntable (available at hardware stores). The turntable will double your space.

Skin Do's

Getting rid of a blemish

- Rub a styptic pencil (used for razor cuts) on a pimple three times a day and it will dry up quickly.

Vinegar astringent
● All you need is one-quarter cup of apple-cider vinegar, one-half cup of water, and one teaspoon of cream of tartar. Mix cream of tartar with water. Add vinegar. Shake thoroughly. Apply with cotton pads. You must shake this formula before each use.

Deep pore mask
● Grind about two ounces of blanched almonds in the blender, then add just enough witch hazel to the powdered almond meal to form a thick paste. Before applying, open pores by steaming your face with a washcloth wrung out with hot water. Leave mask on for fifteen minutes. Rinse with cool water.

Moisturizing mask
● Beat one teaspoon of mayonnaise with one egg yolk. Spread mixture evenly on face. Remove with warm water after twenty minutes. Close pores with a cold-water splash. If you are allergic to the ingredients of the mask, it's not for you.

Make your own bubble bath
● Combine two cups of vegetable oil, three tablespoons of liquid shampoo, and a thimbleful of your favorite perfume. Beat solution in a blender at high speed for several seconds.

Soften hard bath water
● Just add one-half cup of baking soda.

For men only
● Give yourself a facial massage each morning by using an electric razor instead of a blade. It's great for keeping firm, healthy skin and avoiding the jowls that appear as we grow older. Also, rather than shaving lotion, apply a good moisturizing cream so as to lubricate your skin instead of drying it.

Fresh Ideas

Problem perspiration

● If underarm deodorants irritate your skin, no matter how gentle the product, try applying hand cream before the antiperspirant. The lotion won't interfere with the effectiveness of the deodorant.

● Make your own inexpensive and convenient roll-on deodorant by adding two tablespoons of alum (available at drugstores) to one pint of water. Shake mixture well and pour it into a clean, empty roll-on deodorant bottle. (To remove the ball from the bottle, run it under cold water and pry off gently with a nail file.)

Tweezing hints

● Take the pain out of tweezing your eyebrows. Hold the eyebrow between the thumb and index finger and roll firmly for fifteen seconds. This will numb the area and allow you to tweeze in comfort.

● When tweezers won't close firmly, wrap both tips of the tweezers with small rubber bands. The rubber grips better and makes the tweezer more efficient.

● Or apply a commercial product used to numb the gums when a baby is teething.

Pets

K-9 Ideas

Puppy love
- When caring for a litter of puppies or kittens, place them in an old mesh playpen. For pens with wooden slats, tape fine screen around the pen so they don't fall out.
- Put some of your old clothes in puppy's box so he'll pick up your scent and be comforted by it.

Housebreaking
- Hang a bell on the doorknob and jingle it when you want to take puppy outside. He'll soon be jingling it himself when he needs to go out.

Portable dog anchor
- Make a portable dog anchor by tying his leash around an old tire and putting a few bricks inside.

In the doghouse
- Make an entrance flap for a doghouse out of a piece of indoor/outdoor carpeting. Cut it to size, slit it up the middle, and nail it in place.
- Or use a rubber floor mat. Guide your dog through the flap a few times until he learns how to do it himself.

Bathtime
- Fill a tub with warm water and put a rubber mat on the bottom for secure footing.
- Put cotton in your dog's ears to keep out water and a little petroleum jelly around his eyes to protect them from soap.
- Add a little baking soda to the rinse water to make your pet's coat softer, shinier, and odor-free.

- Baking soda or dry cornmeal is a good dry shampoo for any furry pet. Rub it in well, then brush it out. Baking soda is a deodorizer, too.

Quick drying after bathtime
- Use a blow dryer with the temperature set at warm, not hot.

Fleas will flee
- Brewer's yeast rubbed on your dog's coat prevents fleas.

Snow problem
- Snow-melting chemicals may not only be irritating to a dog's paws, but licking at the substance may make him ill. Therefore, wash your dog's feet in a solution of baking soda and water to remove the chemicals.

Chowtime
- Your pet's dish won't slide across the floor while he eats if it's set on a rubber mat.
- Or glue a rubber jar ring to the bottom of his bowl.
- Your dog has a habit of knocking over his water dish? Set an angel-food cake pan over a wooden stake driven into the ground.

"Canned" dog food
- Store big bags of dry dog food in a clean garbage can with a lid.

Let sleeping dogs lie
- If your dog sleeps under your bed, save the time and trouble of removing hair from the box spring by fitting an old contour sheet to the underside. Just wash it when it gets dirty. This is a good idea even if you don't have a pet.

Cat Tales

Finicky felines
- Your cat won't be so choosy if some oil from a can of tuna is sprinkled over his food.
- Or add a teaspoonful of brewer's yeast occasionally. It's healthful because of the B vitamins.

No trespassing
- Keep the cat out of the fishbowl by cutting a square piece of netting (from an orange bag) and securing it over the top of the bowl with a rubber band.
- This also prevents fish from jumping out of the bowl.

Cat Rx
- When your cat refuses liquid medicine, spill some on his fur. He will instinctively lick it off.

A good way to train your cat
- Keep handy a squirt gun filled with water. A few good shots and he'll get the message.

Toys
- Cats love scratching sounds. Crumple a piece of aluminum foil into a ball and let your kitten bat it around on a hard floor.

- Or suspend a Ping-Pong ball on a piece of string from an empty shelf. Cats love to jump up and hit things, and the ball can't roll under the furniture.

Cheaper cat-litter liners
- A box of ten plastic lawn bags makes forty litter-pan liners. Cut each bag into four large rectangular pieces.

Did you know?
- That many cats and dogs go berserk when they hear a violin solo?

Feathers and a Fin

Birdbaths
- Here's how you coax birds into the birdbath: Put some sand on the bottom and a few seeds on the surface of the water.
- And if it's in the sun, move it to the shade. The water may be too warm.
- Get rid of birdbath fungus. Soak some towels in bleach and place them on the sides of the empty bath for half an hour. Remove the towels and rinse both thoroughly.

Keeping squirrels out of a bird feeder
- Cut a hole in the bottom of a plastic wastebasket and slide it upside down on the pole that holds the feeder.

"Cheep" birdseed
- Dried seeds from melons, pumpkins, or squash make great birdseed.

- Transfer birdseed from the original box to an empty salt carton for easy pouring.

When your bird flies the coop
- Turn off the lights and close the drapes. A bird will normally stay motionless in the dark until you can catch him.

Cleaning fish tanks
- Soap should never be used to clean fish tanks. Use nylon netting and noniodized table salt. Rinse tank well to remove all residue.

Sewing

Needles and Thread

Finding the eye of the needle

- Hold an index card behind a machine needle to help you find the eye.
- When threading yarn, put a piece of tape or paper around the end and snip it at a slant. The yarn will fit easily through the needle eye.

Thread lines

- Because thread usually lightens, it's wise to buy thread a little bit darker than the material you're working with.
- To keep a bobbin and matching thread together, run a pipe cleaner through both, then twist.

Buttons and Zippers

Loose buttons

- Touch the center of the button (front and back) with clear nail polish if a button comes loose and you can't repair it right away.
- Or to hold the threads temporarily, put a small strip of transparent tape on them.

Storing buttons

- A handy place to keep extra buttons is with the pattern.
- When removing buttons from a soon-to-be-discarded item, sew them together before storing with your spares. It'll save you the time of having to match buttons later.
- Find buttons easily. Sort them by size or color in the compartments of an egg carton.

Right on the button

- Keep the buttons in place while you stitch: After positioning each button for a shirt, tape them onto the fabric with transparent tape.
- When covering a button with a sheer fabric, the job will be neater if you first cover the button with wool or flannel.

- To avoid cutting into the fabric when snipping off a button, slide a comb between the button and the cloth.

Buttonholes
- Make sample strips of different-sized buttonholes with an automatic buttonholer. Match the button to the sample size when trying to decide which size buttonhole to make.
- When cutting buttonholes by machine, mark the ends of the hole with straight pins to avoid cutting too far.
- To hide interfacing that shows along the edge of a buttonhole, color it with a marking pen to match the fabric.
- Sew the buttonholes horizontally when making children's clothing and they'll be less likely to pop open while they play.

Zippers
- Zippers will be easier to sew if you tape the zipper in place and stitch next to (*not through*) the tape. The tape can be pulled off easily after the zipper is sewn.
- If zipper teeth are broken near the bottom, sew that end closed and make the zipper a little shorter.
- For a zipper that just won't stay closed, sew a small button at the top and make a loop of strong thread through the hole in the zipper pull. When you zip up, just hook the loop over the button.

Patterns and Fabric

Storing patterns
- Your favorite patterns will last longer if you put them in manila envelopes or locking plastic bags.
- The cut-out pieces of a pattern will stay smoother if you hang them on a clamp-type skirt hanger instead of folding them.
- Avoid losing pieces of your pattern as you sew: Clip the pieces together with a spring-action clothespin.

Repairing patterns
- Use a strip of plastic freezer paper to repair a torn pattern. Place a torn section over the freezer paper and press with a warm iron.

Homemade patterns
- Look through a children's coloring book for simple, decorative outlines for quilt patterns.

- Use a coloring book that features your youngster's favorite movie or television character to make a novelty print for a T-shirt or pajama top. Trace the picture onto the garment with tracing carbon, then color it in with ballpoint fabric paint (available at craft stores).
- The peel-away backings from adhesive shelf paper, which are ruled in one-inch squares, make handy guides for enlarging your needlework patterns.

Storing fabric scraps
- Take a plastic garbage can with a lid. Tape a small sample of each piece of fabric to the lid. Now, when you need a certain type of fabric, you can check the lid instead of having to rummage through the whole can.

Sewing Tools
and Tricks

Sewing tools
- A child's game board makes a great sewing board. Put it on your lap when pinning, marking, or cutting.
- For convenience, glue a tape measure to the front edge of your sewing machine.
- A small magnet glued to the end of a yardstick makes it easy to retrieve dropped pins and needles without having to bend.
- Keep a nutpick in your sewing basket. The blunt end is perfect for turning belts, and the sharp end can be used to pull out corners after the belt is turned.

Hemming ways

- To eliminate the white hemline mark after letting down a pair of blue jeans, rub a matching blue crayon on the line and iron the fabric under a pressing cloth, using medium heat.
- Try hair clips instead of basting or pinning a hem in place.
- Before dying a garment, baste a few strands of white thread through it. When finished, remove the threads and wrap them around a spool for future mending or hemming.
- Thread a few needles with basic-colored thread and keep them in a safe, handy place near your washing machine. If you spot a loose hem or a small tear, fix it before you wash the item.

The best way to hem curtains

- Shorten them at the top instead of at the bottom. No one will notice if your job isn't perfect.

"Darn" it all

- Stick a straight wooden clothespin inside the finger of gloves that need mending.
- A ragged hole or tear will be easier to darn if you pull the fabric together as much as possible and iron it between two pieces of waxed paper.
- To repair a hole in a bulky-knit fabric, use the plastic L'Eggs panty-hose egg for a darning surface.

Let's patch things up

- Get the most wear out of your youngster's play pants by turning them inside out and ironing patches on the seat and knees.

Sewing seams

- Always pin across a seam, never parallel with it. That way you can sew over the pins.
- To join straight and bias material smoothly, keep the bias on top.

A pocketful of sense

- A piece of cardboard placed inside the pocket when mending it prevents your needle from catching the other side.
- Use the same color material to make the pockets as that of the slacks. Unsightly white pocket lining won't show every time you sit.
- When sewing the pocket on a new garment, reinforce the top corners with a small piece of the fabric sewn on the inside.

Three cheers for Velcro fasteners
- Velcro fasteners are handy for fastening felt letters and emblems to cheerleaders' outfits. Emblems won't have to be removed and resewn every time you wash the garments, and one set of emblems can be used for several different uniforms.
- Put Velcro fasteners in strategic spots on a wraparound skirt and both waist and hemline will stay even.
- To prevent insulated drapes from gapping between panels, sew strips of Velcro fasteners on adjacent panel hems. Drapes will stay neatly and firmly closed, and keep cold air from entering the room.

Centering pant creases perfectly
- After cutting out slacks pattern, place the front pieces of the material on an ironing board and fold to press a crease. Press with a steam iron on a damp cloth.

This hint is a keeper
- For badly worn collars, take out the stitching at the neck seam and carefully remove the collar, then turn it around and sew it back in. The collar will look like new.

Slide-proof comforter
- Sew a piece of muslin across the bottom of a satin quilt or comforter and tuck that part under the mattress. The comforter won't slide around the bed anymore.

Special Occasions

Wrap-ups

Storing wrapping paper
- Simplify storing and gift wrapping by placing rolled wrapping paper in a tall, narrow wastebasket. Tape a bag to the side to hold tape, scissors, pen, and labels.

How much wrapping paper?
- Wrap a string around the package and measure it, allowing a couple of extra inches for overlap. Use the string to measure the wrapping paper before cutting.

For easy paper cutting
- Pull apart a table with leaves, lay the paper over the slit, and cut with a sharp knife or a single-edged razor.

Making used wrapping paper and ribbon new again
- Wrinkled paper perks back to life! Lightly spritz the wrong side with a little spray starch, then press it with a warm iron.
- Run wrinkled ribbon through a warm curling iron.

Cut to ribbons
- Make your own ribbon by cutting almost any type of fabric into the desired width and length. Striped material is perfect to cut in even widths. Press between sheets of waxed paper with a hot iron. The wax keeps the strips from unraveling and provides enough stiffness for the ribbon to hold its shape when made into a bow.

A handy string dispenser
- Make a hole in the center of a L'Eggs panty-hose container lid and thread the string through the hole.

Original gift wrapping

- Wrap a going-away gift in a large, colorful map.
- A striped kitchen towel makes a great covering for a kitchen shower gift. Instead of decorating the package with a bow, attach a plastic or copper scouring pad or colorful plastic measuring spoons.
- Use a receiving blanket and diaper pins for baby shower gifts.
- Select the newspaper section related to the gift you're giving. Use the real estate section for a housewarming gift.
- The *Wall Street Journal* is ideal for wrapping a book about finances.

- Try sheet music for your musically minded friends.
- The comic strips are perfect for the kids; decorate the package with lollipops or candy canes. How about topping off a Christmas package with a gingerbread man?
- Attach fresh flowers to the bow, but first wrap the stems in damp paper towels and cover them with foil.

Mailing a wrapped present

- Stuff plastic dry-cleaner bags with crumpled newspaper. Use as buffers when packing and newsprint won't rub off on the wrapping paper.
- Protect the bow from being crushed by covering it with a plastic berry basket (like the ones strawberries come in).

Many happy returns

- Always ask the salesperson for two receipts—one for you with the price, the other one with the description of the gift but without the price. Enclose the last one with the gift just in case it has to be returned.

It's the thought that counts

- When your children receive a gift, take a picture of them playing with it or wearing it and send it as a thank-you note.

Inexpensive Gift Ideas

Great expectations
- As soon as you know a friend is expecting a baby, start a scrapbook of current events. Fill it with clippings of news headlines, fashion photos, food and movie ads, pictures of cars and famous people. The final page can be left for the front page of the newspaper on the day the baby is born.
- For the father-to-be, give a waiting-room kit. Fill a box with change for the telephone, telephone numbers of close relatives and friends, cigars, gum, lighter, his favorite magazine, and whatever else you can think of to keep him busy.

The buck pops here
- The kids will love this one. Roll up a dollar bill and insert it into a balloon. Mail it along in a card with instructions to blow up and pop.
- Or insert an invitation to a party with the same instructions to blow up and pop.

Unexpected bonus
- When a friend requests a special recipe, you can turn it into a special occasion by giving one of the expensive ingredients along with a copy of the recipe: a bottle of wine for beef Burgundy, wild rice for a favorite casserole, or shrimp for a dip.

For the new bride
● Fill an address book with addresses and phone numbers of relatives and friends, and add a special section for birthdays and anniversaries.

The gift of gab
● Telephone companies offer gift certificates they will mail to whomever you wish. This is a perfect way to let friends and relatives know that you'd love to hear from them. The recipient simply mails in the coupon in place of money with the monthly telephone bill. Call your local phone company for more information.

Party Plans

Housewarming party
● If you're expecting guests who have never been to your new home, put a colored light bulb in your yard or porch fixture and tell them to look for it.

Anniversary greeting
● Make your own greeting card in a flash by taking a snapshot of the family holding a sign saying "Happy Anniversary" or any other message.

Bridal shower
● It's fun to have each guest bring her favorite recipe, along with a utensil used for preparing the dish. For example, a Chinese recipe with a wok, an omelet recipe with an omelet pan, a meat-loaf recipe with a loaf pan. The hostess could provide the bride-to-be with a recipe box to store all her new recipes.

Special dinners
● Polish your sterling in advance and wrap it in airtight plastic bags to prevent tarnishing.
● Don't forget to spray your prized linen tablecloth with either spray starch or fabric protector. Spills will be easier to remove.

Celebrating a job promotion
- Bring out the champagne. But if you don't drink it all, here's a way to keep it bubbly for a week longer. Drop a stainless-steel turkey skewer into the bottle and fasten a balloon over the neck with a rubber band. This will trap the carbonation.
- Lost the cork to a wine bottle? Soften a candle stub, wrap it in paper toweling and insert it into the neck of the bottle.

Birthday party
- It's easy to serve punch in a thirty-cup coffee maker. Remove the basket and there's plenty of room for ice.
- Make your ice cubes in advance. After they're frozen, store them in brown paper bags and they won't stick together.

Outdoor fish fry
- You're having a large crowd and want to serve everyone at once? As you fry the fish put them in a Styrofoam cooler lined with paper toweling and put the lid on. Fish will stay hot.

Pool parties
- Make your own coconut cream for piña coladas by pureeing three cups of chopped coconut in a blender with a little boiling water. Squeeze liquid through cheesecloth.

Family picnic
- Bring along a small, lightweight wagon. Load it up with blankets, lawn chairs, and the picnic basket for the trip from the parking spot to the picnic area.

- Fill plastic bags that seal three-quarters full of water and place in the freezer. If your family decides on a picnic at the last minute, just toss a few bags into the cooler to keep food cold. To make small pieces of ice for soft drinks, just hit with a hammer.
- Cut the legs off an old card table to make a perfect picnic table for the beach.

Barbecue
- Use a muffin pan to hold the fixings, such as mustard, catsup, relish, and onions. You won't have to pass around a lot of bottles and jars.
- A sure way to start a charcoal fire: Punch a few holes in the sides of a coffee can, remove both ends, and set it in the grill. Fill with charcoal, add starter fluid and light. When the coals are glowing, remove the can with tongs and set it in a safe place. Spread the coals and replace the grill.
- Keep a few flower pots filled with sand near smokers and stop worrying about their littering the lawn.

Candlelight dinners
- Thin candles won't stand up? Twist a rubber band around the candle base before inserting it into the holder.
- Or keep candles firmly in place with a little florist's clay in the holder.
- Is your candle too large for the holder? Trim the excess with a hot, sharp knife.
- Large, round candles can split and crumble when pressed onto the spike of a holder. Avoid this by making a hole in the bottom of the candle with a hot nail.
- When candles become dull and lose their newness, spray furniture polish on a cloth and wipe them thoroughly. They'll look new again.

Winter get-togethers
- Dazzle your guests—line your driveway with weatherproof lights. Here's how: Save plastic gallon ice-cream containers and coat the inside with vegetable spray. Fill with water and set outside. When partially frozen, insert a thick candle in the center and freeze solid. Remove from container. Light and line your driveway or walk.

Christmas Tree-trimming
- Always buy a fresh tree and check to see if the trunk has been sealed. If it has, you must cut off the bottom before placing it in water to help the tree absorb moisture. The cut should be diagonal, about two inches from the bottom.

- And to help your tree stay fresh longer, drill a hole up through the bottom of the trunk as far as you can, then stuff with strips of sponge. The sponge acts like a wick to soak up water and carry it deeper into the trunk.
- When assembling an artificial tree, dip the ends of the branches in petroleum jelly before inserting into the frame.
- To remove tree pitch from your hands, rub them with salad oil and wipe with a paper towel.

Decorating the tree
- When different strings of tree lights are all tangled together, try this hint: Plug in one set and, by following the lights, untangle one string at a time.
- If you're stringing popcorn on the tree, pop the corn a week ahead of time. The stale kernels will slide onto the needle without breaking.
- Use green pipe cleaners to tie tree lights to the branches.
- Stiffen crocheted Christmas ornaments with a few shots of hair spray.
- A few small bells hung low on the tree will announce that little fingers or paws are busy there.

Taking the tree down
- To prevent tangled tree lights, store them around empty gift-wrap tubes. Push the plug into the tube, then wrap the lights around the outside and secure the end with a rubber band. Several strings of lights can be stored on the same tube.
- Wrap one or two old bed sheets around the tree like a sling and needles won't drop on the carpet. You'll need another person to help you carry it out. Go through the door trunk first.

New Year's Eve
- Here's a nifty way to make your own inexpensive liqueur for the big night. Combine one pound of dried apricots, peaches, or pears, one cup of superfine sugar, and one quart of inexpensive vodka in a large jar. Shake well to dissolve sugar. Cover and let stand for one week, shaking the contents daily. Strain liqueur into a decanter. The fruit can be served over ice cream or cake.
- Make your own superfine sugar from granulated by processing in a blender at high speed.

Part III

Away from Home

The Car

Car Cues

Neater car washes
- All you need are two buckets of water and three Turkish towels. Put soapy water in one bucket, clear water in the other. Start with the roof and work your way down, one section at a time. Use one towel and soapy water to wash, the second towel and clear water to rinse, and the third towel to dry. You'll end up with a clean, dry car instead of a mess.

Three ways for washdays
- On hot, sunny days, wash and wax your car in the shade or at dusk. This will prevent streaking.
- A dust-mop head, worn as a mitten, is great for spreading suds and loosening grime.
- Or use carpet scraps glued to a block of wood.

The shining
- Sprinkle a tablespoon of cornstarch on the wipe rag when buffing your car and excess polish will come off easily.
- Or, for a glittering final finish to a newly waxed car, spray it down with cold water, then towel-dry it.
- Give windows and chrome a super shine by polishing with newspaper.

Interior information
- Wipe vinyl seats and dashboards with a cloth dampened with self-stripping floor-wax cleaner. It removes dirt and also covers scratches and scuffs. Quickly dries to a nonsticky shine.
- Or try a solution of three tablespoons of washing soda and one quart of warm water.
- For those stubborn tar spots on auto carpeting, apply Spray 'n Wash; scrub with an old toothbrush.
- Put floor mats in the washing machine with a few old towels to get them extra clean.

Rust-proofing
- Prevent rust by keeping your car clean—outside, inside, and underneath. Set a lawn sprinkler under the car and turn the water on full blast. This washes off the salt and other chemicals that collect on the car bottom during winter.

- Chipped paint spots? Promptly clean the area thoroughly and apply a coat of clear nail polish to prevent rust.
- Aluminum foil dipped in cola will help remove rust spots from car bumpers.

A new tar remover
- Laundry prewash takes tar off car finishes.

Tires
- Steel-wool soap pads and elbow grease still clean whitewall tires best.
- Test how much tread is left in a tire. Stick a penny in the groove. If you can see all of Lincoln's head, there's too little tread.
- Putting air in your tires should be postponed until absolutely necessary when the temperature is 10 degrees or colder. The valve in the tire may freeze and let all the air out.

Windshield wipers
- When wipers begin to wear down, extend their life by rubbing briskly with sandpaper.
- When dirty wipers streak your windshield, give them a good scrubbing with baking soda and water.

Antenna
- A radio antenna will slide easily if a coat of wax is applied occasionally.
- Or rub it occasionally with waxed paper.

Battery "cents"
- Grease one side of a penny and place that side down on the middle of the battery. Corrosion will collect on the penny instead of on the battery posts.
- Or spray the battery terminals with spray paint.

Repairing seat covers

- Increase the market value of your car. See the Yellow Pages under "vinyl repair" and have those little rips and cigarette burns fixed before selling it.
- For home repair use cement glue and a piece of doubleknit material in the same color as the car seat. Work the glued material under the rip until the material surfaces are flat and wrinkle-free. Close the rip and lay a heavy book on top of it until the glue is thoroughly dry.

The silent treatment

- When silicone spray is not available, try silencing a squeaky car door by putting a few drops of transmission fluid on the door hinge with the dipstick.

Trunk take-alongs

- Gloves. Wear them when filling the tank at a self-service station or when changing a tire.
- An old window shade. Unrolled, it serves as a mat to protect clothing if you have to change a tire.
- A bleach bottle. Cut it in half. The top makes a free funnel.
- Reflector tape. Cover a burned-out headlight with it until you can get to a service station.
- A squeeze bottle filled with club soda or cola. Nothing is better for removing grease buildup from the windshield. A must when traveling long distances.
- Baking soda and plastic net bags (the kind onions come in). Sprinkle onion bags with baking soda and rub headlights to remove salt residue in winter. You can also use the onion bags to clear insects from the headlights and windshield.
- A broom with the handle cut down. It's the quickest way to brush snow off a car.
- A piece of plastic rug protector. It's great for lining the trunk to protect against grease smudges and spills.

Glove compartment handies

- Use moistened hand wipes to remove gas odor from your hands after you've filled the tank at a self-service gas station.
- Toss in a few dimes and you'll always have change for a highway telephone booth.

Stash this under the seat

- A large plastic trash bag makes a fine emergency raincoat.

Another tape-reflector hint

- For extra safety put strips of reflector tape on the door sill of the driver's door. When the door is opened, the reflection will alert drivers approaching from the rear.

Wash your hands with these

- Remove auto grease with baking soda and water.
- Or give your hands a good scrubbing with Lux liquid detergent.
- Or, before working on your car, rub dishwashing detergent on hands, elbows, and under fingernails. Let it dry but don't wipe it off. The soap seals pores against dirt and grease. When the job is finished, just wash up with soap and water and your hands will come clean.

Emergency substitutes

- Use a hubcap as a shovel if your car gets stuck in snow, sand, or mud.
- Out of gas? If you have no funnel to pour gasoline from a can, use a map, newspaper, or paper bag to guide the gas into the tank. Don't light a match.
- Your radiator needs water and you're not near a hose? Carry the water in the windshield-washer jug or the radiator-overflow jug.
- Cover a partially used one-quart can of motor oil with the plastic lid from a one-pound coffee can.

Locked out without a coat hanger

- Pull out your oil dipstick, wipe it clean, and push the round end between the rubber door seal and the window. Keep maneuvering until the end catches the lock, then lift.

Better tune-ups

- If you gap your own plugs, use the widest gap that the manufacturer recommends and your car will run better, idle better, and give you better mileage.

Garage floors

- Spread cat litter on garage floors to catch oil drips. Just sweep it up when it becomes saturated.
- Or try to purchase from a friendly service station a sweeping compound that absorbs grease.
- Use a prewash spray to remove grease spots. Spray on prewash and let it stand five minutes. Sprinkle on powdered detergent, scrub with a broom, and hose off.

- Before sweeping out a dirty garage, shred some newspaper and dampen with hot water. To prevent dust from rising and resettling as you sweep, first spread the moist pieces on the floor as you would a sweeping compound.
- Or try fresh grass clippings.

Parking precautions
- Hang a tire at bumper height on the front end of your garage.
- If garage space is tight, put strips of inner tube, foam rubber, or carpeting on the side walls, where your car door hits when opened.

Avoid the hot seat
- When you park in the sun in the summer, cover the car seat and back with a towel.

Frost foilers
- Keep car windows free of ice overnight or for any extended period of time by spreading a sheet of heavy-duty plastic (available at hardware stores) over the windshield. Catch one end inside the door on the driver's side, and secure the other end inside the passenger door.
- Leave one window open a crack to prevent frost from building up on the inside of the windows.

Saving money on auto repairs
- Save up to 50 percent on auto repairs, paint jobs, and engine work by checking with auto-repair schools in your area.

- Most paint shops reduce the cost of painting your car if you remove all trim, door handles, and mirrors yourself.

Before buying a used car
- Call this toll-free government number—800-424-9393—and find out if the car you're interested in has ever been recalled.
- Don't buy a used car on a rainy day. All cars with dull or blemished finishes look better when they are wet.

No butts about it
- To keep passengers from smoking, give them the message by filling your ashtray with change for tolls or wrapped hard candy.

Travel

Pack Facts

Packing an airtight case
- When packing shampoo, mouthwash, and liquid cosmetics in plastic bottles, squeeze the bottle and force out some of the air just before tightening the cap. This creates a partial vacuum and helps prevent leakage.
- Make a handy toothbrush container from a plastic pill bottle. Cut a slit in the top, slip the handle through it, and snap it back on the bottle with the bristles inside.
- Instead of traveling with a bottle of nail-polish remover, which might leak in your suitcase, saturate several cotton balls with the remover and keep them in a small, airtight jar.

Uses for locking plastic bags
- Use them to hold shoes to protect surrounding clothing.
- A large size will hold dirty laundry.
- They'll keep stationery and stamps clean.
- They'll prevent bottles of liquid medication, hair spray, and perfumes from leaking. (Use the kind that seal.)

Don't forget these if you're staying in a hotel
- A long extension cord. It won't matter then where the mirror or outlets are in the room.
- High-wattage light bulb. Just in case you need more light when applying makeup or reading.
- Water heater and instant coffee or tea. No more waiting for room service.
- Several clip-type clothespins for clipping slacks and skirts to ordinary hangers.

Do not disturb
● Hang the DO NOT DISTURB sign on your motel or hotel room door when you leave for the evening and chances are you won't have any unwanted guests.

On call
● Two wake-up calls are better than one. The first may be overlooked or you could fall asleep again.

Save on crib rental
● Take along a heavy-duty, flat cardboard box. Set up the box on the floor and line the bottom with a heavy, quilted blanket. The high sides will keep drafts off baby.

Air "Lines"

Nonstop or direct flights
● Be aware of the difference between nonstop and direct flights when booking your reservation. Nonstop flights don't stop. Direct flights, however, may stop many times between your departure and your destination. "Direct" simply means that you don't change planes at a stopover.

For cabin fever
● Airplane-cabin pressurization causes dehydration, so drink a glass of water every hour and you'll feel better when you arrive.
● Wear loose clothing (such as a jogging suit) and shoes because the body tends to swell at an altitude of more than five thousand feet.

Baggage checks
● Put identification tags on both the outside and the inside of suitcases. Bags without outside tags will be opened after three days if they haven't been claimed.
● Never use curbside baggage-checking service. It increases the odds that your luggage will be lost or delayed.
● Most lost luggage is checked in less than a half hour before flight time. So check in early.
● Watch to make sure that each bag is tagged and sent on the conveyor belt or it could be left sitting there.

Quick luggage identification
- Tie brightly colored yarn to the handles of your luggage and you'll be able to identify your bag quickly.

Replacing a broken suitcase handle
- Use a dog collar looped through the metal rings.
- Replace with a dog leash the lost strap used to pull luggage on wheels.

Flying with kids
- Give baby a bottle or pacifier at takeoff and landing to reduce pressure on ears.
- Have hard candy or gum ready for the older kids.
- And remember, a few glasses of cola have as much caffeine as a cup of coffee. Don't give them to the kids if you want them to sleep.

Inspections
- If you are traveling with a gift-wrapped package, wrap the lid and the box separately so the lid can be removed for inspection at the airport. (Use rubber bands to hold the lid on.)

Over there . . .
- When traveling in foreign countries, always carry your hotel matchbook with you. If you get lost, local residents can help you find your way back.
- And carry picture postcards of the places you'd like to visit. Show the cards to cab drivers and there'll be no confusion getting to the right spot.
- Pack a large, collapsible canvas suitcase in the bottom of one of your suitcases in case you go on a shopping spree. When returning from abroad, put all declarable items in one bag and maybe you'll save time going through customs.

Medical standbys

- It's not a bad idea to carry a spare pair of eyeglasses when traveling abroad, and take along a copy of the prescription when traveling in the United States.
- When traveling with prescription drugs, make sure they are in the original containers. Also, carry a copy of the prescription in case you need a refill or have some explaining to do at customs.
- Make note of the generic name of each medicine, since brand names differ in foreign countries.
- Try earplugs and an eyeshade if you can't sleep on planes and trains.

Cameras

- When taking new, expensive, foreign-made cameras, watches, and recorders out of the United States, register them with the U.S. customs before you leave. This way, you can't be asked to pay duty on them when you return.
- Remember that airport security X-ray scanning devices in many foreign countries are more powerful than those in the United States, and may ruin your film. Always unload your camera before passing it through inspection. (Many foreign airports insist on passing the camera through the machine; in the United States you have the right to have it inspected by hand.)

Cruise control
- Remember this general rule for boat cruises: The shorter the cruise, the younger the passengers.

Road "Ways"

Map your route
- After deciding on the route you'll be taking, mark it on the map with a felt-tipped pen.

Saving space and trouble
- Pack bedding in drawstring laundry bags. The bags hold a lot without taking up much space, and they can double as pillows in the backseat for the kids.
- You won't have to empty the whole trunk to get to the jack if you pack it last.

For fast cleanups
- Fill a plastic liquid-detergent bottle (without rinsing it out) with water and keep it in the glove compartment with paper towels.

Keeping the kids busy
- Pack a scrapbook, scissors, and glue. At night the children can paste the day's collection of postcards, menus, and other memorabilia into the scrapbook. The book will not only help with school reports on "What I Did This Summer" but will keep the kids busy collecting souvenirs during the day.
- Bring along a couple of jump ropes so the kids can work off excess energy whenever you stop for food or gas.

Wish you were here
- If you plan to send postcards while on vacation, put all the addresses on sticker labels before you go instead of carrying an address book.

Surefire
Camping Hints

Fast food
- Prepare some of the food as far in advance as possible, then seal in locking food storage bags. At the campsite, heat the bags and use the same water to wash dishes.

Fast ways to do laundry
- On camping trips use a clean plunger as an agitator and a plastic bucket as a washtub when doing small laundry jobs.
- Or put dirty clothes, detergent, and water in a large container with a tight-fitting lid. Set it in your car trunk, and while you're driving to the next campsite the dirty clothes will be swishing around and cleaning themselves.

Keeping your trailer hitch rust-free
- Cut a slit in a tennis ball and fit it snugly over the hitch ball. This will keep it dry and rust-free.

Flashlights
- Put a piece of tape over the flashlight switch so it won't get turned on accidentally in the suitcase.
- Protect your flashlight in the rain. Put it in a plastic sandwich bag and close the opening with a rubber band. You can turn it on and off without removing it, and the light shines brightly through the plastic.

Matches
- Wrap kitchen matches in aluminum foil to keep them dry on fishing, camping, and other outdoor trips.

Fishing-trip tips
- Keep your fishing license in an old ballpoint pen. Remove the cartridge, roll up the license, and stuff it inside the pen. Toss it in your tackle box or clip it to your shirt pocket.

- Ever try to pull a worm from the bottom of the can? Take a can with a plastic top and cut out both ends. Put plastic covers on each. When you want a worm, open up the end where it is.

- Wrap a triple thickness of aluminum foil around the hook immediately after taking the rod out of the water. The hook won't stick anybody or get tangled up with other rods in the boat.

This hint gets an A or a B
- Make a note of your blood type on your driver's license in case of an emergency.

Storing suitcases
- To keep suitcases smelling fresh, store them with a fabric-softener sheet or a bar of scented soap inside.
- Or store suitcases with a small packet of activated charcoal (available at your florist) or crumpled-up newspaper inside to avoid musty odors.

For those little worries you can laugh about
- When slacks or jeans are too tight to close easily, lie down and zip them up.
- You have trouble getting your children into the tub? Tell them that the last one to take a bath must clean it.
- If you have a garage sale, don't mark prices on the items; let people make you an offer. Often it'll be more than you would have charged.
- When finally you find something after looking all over the house for it, put it back in the first place you looked. That's probably where it belongs.
- To eliminate the mess from cigarettes and cut down on the alcohol bill, invite a clergyman to your party.
- If you need a little help getting that ear-bending friend off the telephone, make a cassette recording of some background noises. Doorbell sounds and children crying are good for starters.
- If you're still in bed when your husband walks through the front door at the end of the day, dab a little liquid cleaner behind each ear. It'll make you smell as if you've been housecleaning all day and deserve dinner out.
- When your house is so messy that you want to throw up your hands in despair, just take off your glasses and things won't look so bad.
- Maybe your kids will brush their teeth without trouble if you tell them the Tooth Fairy pays a lot more for healthy teeth.
- To get children to eat cereal with less sugar, put sugar in a salt shaker.
- If you want to eat less, use chopsticks or eat in front of a mirror.
- When you find yourself in charge of a group of children, have them understand that whoever says, "Me first," is automatically last.

- Your cat will eat only the food from expensive small cans? Try mixing in a little of the less expensive food that comes in the larger cans. Gradually increase the cheaper brand until the cat will eat it without turning up its tail.
- If you want your children to begin helping you with household duties, play the "waiter and waitress" game. Mommy and Daddy are the customers.
- The best way to ensure that your dinner guests will enjoy what you serve is to keep them waiting until they're good and hungry.
- If you can't seem to get your kids to clean up after themselves, hide everything you pick up in a secret place and charge a dime an item as ransom.
- Your hungry mate is due home from work any minute and you haven't started dinner yet! Sauté an onion in a little oil. He'll come home, smell "food" cooking, and won't realize that dinner is going to be late.
- To train children not to complain or tattle, give them a limited supply of complaint tickets. Each time they have a complaint they must give you a ticket before you will listen. The child will have to think twice before using up one of his complaints.
- Chronicle your first year of marriage in a diary because by your tenth anniversary, if you have had children, you will swear that in your entire married life you haven't had ten whole minutes alone.
- Your husband has been complaining about the messy house? Re-arrange the furniture and he'll think you've been scrubbing all day.
- If you want to be discreet about the number of birthday candles on a cake, your own for instance, place them in the form of a question mark.
- When a toddler hates to leave the tub, pull the plug.

- Don't make staying in bed too much fun for a child who is ill. You might delay recovery.
- When you're sick, keep a police whistle near your bed to call your husband.

- And remember, one good turn gets the blanket.

Index